A-Z OF THEMES

RESOURCE BOOK FOR TEACHERS

SHIRLEY SYDENHAM   RON THOMAS

M

First published 1990 by
THE MACMILLAN COMPANY OF AUSTRALIA PTY LTD
107 Moray Street, South Melbourne 3205
6 Clarke Street, Crows Nest 2065
Reprinted 1990

Associated companies
and representatives throughout the world

National Library of Australia
cataloguing in publication data

Sydenham, Shirley.
  A–Z of themes.

  Includes index.
  ISBN 0 7329 0086 7.

  1. Primary school teaching. 2. Teaching — Aids and
  devices. 3. Education, Primary — Activity programs.
  I. Thomas, Ron, 1947–   II. Title.

372.13078

Set in Univers by Setrite Typesetters, Hong Kong
Printed in Hong Kong

Contents

Introduction

In *A—Z of Themes* you will find more than thirty themes which are designed for use in classrooms from Kindergarten to Year 8. While they are not graded in any way, in each theme you will find activities which can be used at many levels. The ideas can be adapted by the classroom teacher to suit particular age groups, and individuals within those age groups.

In components of *A—Z of Themes* you will find ideas for science, mathematics, drama, art, and so on. Thus, *A—Z of Themes* supports an integrated curriculum approach to teaching.

Cross referencing enables one theme to be linked to another and activities from within each theme can be incorporated into another. For example, how to make a phenakistoscope is detailed in the theme Zoetropes, but the activity could be considered for inclusion in other themes, for example Astronomy. There are many such references made in *A—Z of Themes*.

The detailed index provides references to specific skills and activities, and bibliographies at the end of each theme provide literature and expository text references.

A—Z of Themes is a starting point for thematic study in the classroom. It advocates integration of traditional curriculum areas and the synthesis of reading, writing, speaking and listening.

It is not an exhaustive list of activities to be included in any thematic study. But, it is a beginning.

Be flexible!
resourceful!
inventive!
creative!
and allow children to be likewise . . . .

The following symbols are included throughout the text as a guide to different activities:

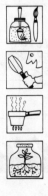

Art

Research

Cooking

Science

Drama

Reading

Games

Writing

Astronomy and Astronauts

Introducing Space

To begin the theme collect and borrow relevant materials such as books, charts, pictures, and science fiction in both comic and book form.
Display, read, listen, discuss and observe.

Planet Environments
Research (in groups) the environment on each of the planets. Find out about the atmosphere, the number of satellites and any special features such as rings. Groups report their findings in a mini-lecture.

Use models of the planets, maps, and dioramas to illustrate a lecture, or as props in a play about a mission to the planet.

Solar System Mobile
Make a mobile of the solar system using polystyrene balls.

Solar System Map
Make a map of the solar system. Use a grid system and show relative distances and sizes to scale.

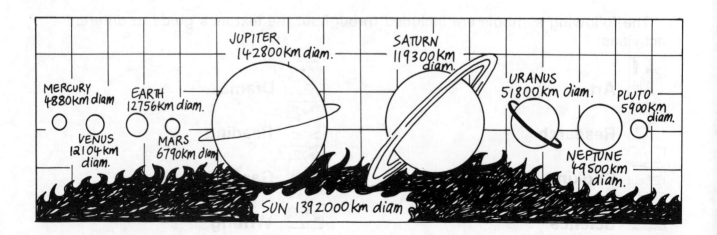

MERCURY 4880km diam

VENUS 12104km diam.

EARTH 12756km diam.

MARS 6790km diam.

JUPITER 142800km diam.

SATURN 119300km diam.

URANUS 51800km diam.

NEPTUNE 49500km diam.

PLUTO 5900km diam.

SUN 1392000km diam

Animation

Try animation on video.
Use the models made as the scenery and the account of the mission as the script. (See p. 207)

Space vehicles

Make models of spacecraft, launch vehicles, and planet surface vehicles. Model makers will know how their vehicles work and about the development of the technology.

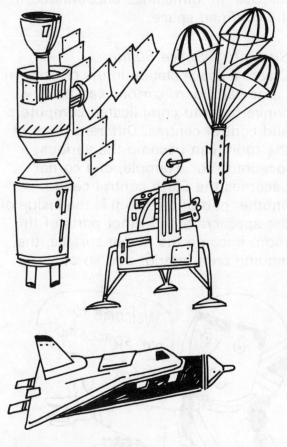

Filmstrip/storyboard

No video?
Make a filmstrip of the voyage and record a commentary.

Research

Read to find out about the training program for astronauts.
- What work do they do in flight? On the planet? In space?
- What do they wear?
- What do they eat?
- How do they do these things: sleep? eat? wash? go to the toilet?
- What are the effects of weightlessness?
- What are the effects of living in a small, confined space?

Create a Space Station

Create a space that is representative of a command module in the classroom. Groups of children can spend time in the space to work, eat lunch and so on. Discuss the difficulties encountered in the confined space.

Simulate a Space Station
Create a space station in the classroom. Large cardboard cartons can be converted into complicated computers and control centres. Different parts of the room can become the various locations. For example, one corner becomes the Earth control centre, another part of the room is the inside of the spacecraft, and other parts of the room become the planet surface, the landing craft interior and so on.

Build the scientific apparatus required in each sector. Make computers out of cardboard cartons. Make dials out of old clock dials, egg carton sections, foil pie plates, parts from old record players and television sets. Cut out sections of the box, cover with coloured cellophane, and put torches inside to create coloured panels.

Record the background noises heard in these locations. Watch some space adventure movies and concentrate on the sound effects used.

In the room, hang UFOs, satellites, planets, stars, comets, meteorites, and other spacecraft.

Welcome to our spaceship!

Create Costumes

Each child can decide on their role in the space environment and design an appropriate costume.

For example, the astronauts exploring the planet will need space helmets and air tanks.

Create costumes for inhabitants of the planet which is being explored, and for a robot used to help the astronauts.

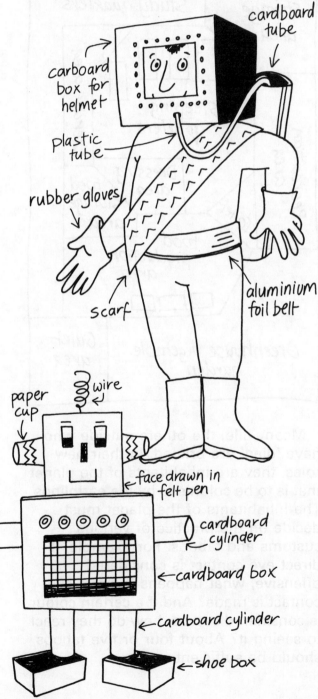

carboard box for helmet

cardboard tube

plastic tube

rubber gloves

scarf

aluminium foil belt

paper cup

wire

face drawn in felt pen

cardboard cylinder

cardboard box

cardboard cylinder

shoe box

Drama: In Space

Warm-up: training session for astronauts — walking, running, hopping, leaping in zero gravity, lifting, pushing, pulling heavy equipment with gravity and without, conducting scientific experiments in zero gravity.

After the warm-up hold a briefing session about a vital mission being sent to a planet to investigate the possibility of establishing an Earth settlement because Earth is over-populated. Children complete Space I.D cards to help establish roles.

Name — photo

Address

Rank/Occupation

Next of kin (to be notified in the event of accident or DEATH)

I.D. No.

'Sleep mode' on spacecraft. Alarm wakes them when they've landed on the planet. Commander (teacher in role) divides them into 3 groups to go to different areas of planet to explore. They are to prepare a 'video transmission' to report their findings, discoveries and adventures. Give groups about 10 minutes to discuss, negotiate and plan this presentation, and then each group can present their scene to the others.

End this session with a discussion about the discoveries, how and where a space station can be built, and what problems could be encountered.

Follow Up Activity

The second session can be the next day or several days later.

In groups of four, children prepare and draw a sequence of about four frozen frames (tableaux). Children are to retain the roles established in the first session. One person in each group is designated as having died in the course of duty since the last session. This person will decide on the manner of his/ her death, and will direct the silent tableaux to show how he/she died. The tableaux are presented as a series of slides or photos. These tableaux are shown to the rest of the grade.

Those who 'died' are taken out of the room. The remainder are equipped with large sheets of paper and crayons or textas, and draw the space station and settlement. The design should include living quarters and areas for working, storage, food production and recreation.

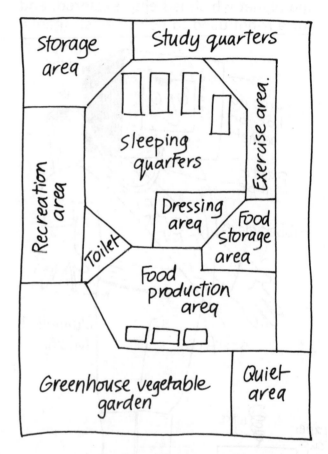

Meanwhile, the others outside who have 'died' are briefed. In their new roles, they are inhabitants of the planet that is to be colonised by the earthlings. The inhabitants of the planet must decide on the practice of various customs and taboos. For example, if direct eye contact is considered offensive, what happens if direct eye contact is made? And if a certain colour is considered sacred, how do they react to seeing it? About four or five taboos should be sufficient.

Back in the classroom, prepare the humans by telling them that you have discovered a community of native inhabitants on the planet, and they are willing to meet. Stress the fact that they are not aggressive and that we humans must try and establish friendly relations. Do not tell them anything else. (Remember: the humans and planet inhabitants don't speak the same language. They will have to find other ways to communicate.)

Bring the two groups together and let them intermingle and try to communicate. After a time, withdraw the inhabitants, and ask the humans if they can work out some of the inhabitants' reactions to the humans' overtures. Let them hypothesise about the correct ways of approach, then bring in the others so that these hypotheses can be tried out.

Discuss with the children how easily they inadvertently offended each other's taboos, the problems of communication and so on.

As a final activity, form groups of four or five, and have each group prepare and present a short scene showing life on that planet twenty years after the human space station was established.

Class Activites

Meet an Alien

In groups or individually, children imagine that they have come into contact with an alien. Draw it. Draw its family portrait. Draw it from different perspectives. Show it running, sleeping, cleaning itself, eating.

Talk or write about feeding it, playing games with it, housing it. What would you do if it hated the people who lived next door?

Body Language

Talk about the 'language' of animals, for example, cats rubbing up against a person's legs, dogs wagging their tails. Invent a body language for your alien. How does it show its feelings?

Book writing

Write a factual information book about the alien. Make it look and read like other information books found in the library and classroom.

Face Painting

Try face painting.
Children use face paints to make their faces into alien faces.

Space Capsule Crash

A space capsule crashes in a remote swamp. It begins to sink. The passengers have only a few moments in which to grab three items each from the space capsule. Children list the items, the reasons why they were chosen, and the usefulness of each item in a survival situation.

Writing

Space Mission

Write an account of the space mission from various points of view:
- of the astronauts who had different jobs to perform, such as the driver of the landing module, the planet surface vehicle driver, the geologist, botanist, and so on.
- the ground controller
- the inhabitants of the planet
- a television news broadcaster
- a newspaper journalist

Write a day by day account in diary form.

Selling a Planet

Prepare a travel brochure to sell the planet as an ideal travel destination. This may involve the planning of a tourist complex on the planet and an itinerary for visiting the attactions.

This could lead on to the selling of real estate, retirement villages, school camp sites and so on.

Space Resident

You are resident on a permanent floating space station. Write letters home, or send postcards. Children will need to draw the pictorial content of the postcard. They will have to invent the stamp. This will lead on to a discussion of other forms of futuristic communication.

Dear Mum,
    We are having a fabulous time here on Space Station 410. The people are very friendly and we are learning a great deal. Yesterday we were part of a scouting party that went to the green planet of Xeron, which was very exciting.
    I'll write again soon,
        love
        Karen
        xxx

More Space Topics

Write about:
- an encounter with an alien
- being marooned in space.

Experiment: Rocket Balloons

On a long balloon, draw (with felt-tipped pens) or paint the features of a rocket ship. Blow up the balloon, twist the mouthpiece and secure with a wooden peg.

On the top side of the balloon, place a drinking straw along the length of the balloon and attach with masking tape. Thread a long piece of string through the straw, and hold it taut across the room. Release the peg and the 'rocket' will fly.

Research:
History of Space Flight

Research, discuss and write about:
- the beginnings of space travel
- early flights
- animals in space
- Russian space flights and achievements
- women in space
- accidents in space
- specific space missions
- lunar landings
- purpose of space exploration
- cost of space exploration
- star wars.

Music

'2001 A Space Odyssey' from Holst 'The Planets'

Bibliography

Ardley, Neil, *Exploring the Universe,* The Universe, Macmillan, London, 1987.

Ardley, Neil, *The Inner Planets*, The Universe, Macmillan, London, 1987.

Ardley, Neil, *The Outer Planets*, The Universe, Macmillan, London, 1987.

Becklake, Sue, *The Mysterious Universe*, Macmillan, 1983.

Bendick, Jeanne, *Space Travel*, Watts, 1982.

Flynn, Randal (ed.), *Your World: Space*, Southern Cross, Macmillan, 1988.

Flynn, Randal, *The History of Space Travel,* Southern Cross, Macmillan, 1987.

Ford, Adam, *Spaceship Earth*, Metheun/Walker, 1971.

Hirst, Robin and Hirst, Sally, *Stargazing Under Southern Stars,* Southern Cross, Macmillan, 1988.

Irvine, Mat, *The Science of the Cosmos*, Macmillan, London, 1985.

Kentzer, Michael, *Space*, Collins, 1979.

McGowen, Tom, *Album of Astronomy*, Rand McNally, 1979.

Moore, Patrick, *The New Challenge of the Stars*, Hutchinson, 1977.

Pollard, Michael, *The Astronaut*, Macmillan, 1972.

Ridpath, Ian, *Outer Space,* The Universe, Macmillan, London, 1987.

Ridpath, Ian , *The Stars,* The Universe, Macmillan, London, 1987.

Ridpath, Ian, *The Sun,* The Universe, Macmillan, London, 1987.

Ryan, Peter, *Journey to the Planets, Penguin, 1972.*

Seevers, James A., Space, Raintree, 1978.

Thomas, Ron and Stutchbury, Jan, *The Sky,* Macmillan Beginners, Macmillan, 1988.

Bees, Bugs and Beetles

Introducing Insects

Begin the theme by collecting specimens of insects from the local environment.

Try the school grounds, the local park, home gardens, a pond or a river.

Encourage children to collect carefully, to replace logs and stones they might turn over, so as to disturb the environment as little as possible. You'll need to take: plastic containers with lids, lifting implements such as a small net, and pen and notebook.

Direct the children to note the type of environment where each creature is found so that it can be recreated inside the classroom 'home'.

FOR CATERPILLARS, APHIDS AND LADYBIRDS:

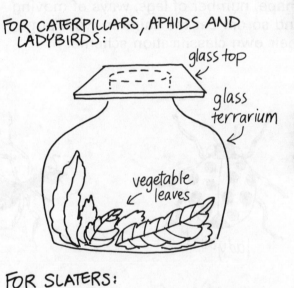

glass top

glass terrarium

vegetable leaves

FOR SLATERS:

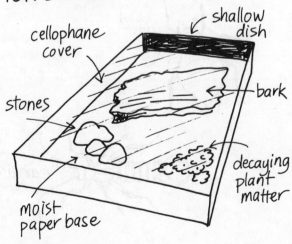

cellophane cover

shallow dish

stones

bark

moist paper base

decaying plant matter

tile

glass jar buried

Small stones

Build a pit trap to catch small insects

Initial Observations

Back in the classroom, make detailed observations of each creature. You'll need magnifying glasses!

Direct children to record:

- shape
- colour
- structure — how many segments?
  does it have a shell?
  how does it move?
  behaviour/habits?

   Make a map showing where each creature was found.

Classification

Animals can be grouped according to size, whether or not they have wings, shape, number of legs, ways of moving and so on. Let the children work out their own classification scheme.

Here's another way.

In the grass we found....

In the trees and bushes we found...

On the building we found...

Under some rocks we found...

In the sand we found...

Under the house we found...

 Word Study: Insect Words

Compile word lists to describe the insects.

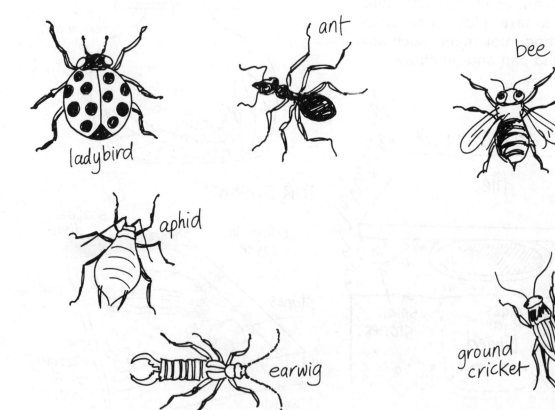

ladybird

ant

bee

aphid

earwig

ground cricket

18

Research: Insects

Measurement
How fast does the creature move?
Graph the results of timing experiments.

How Long?
Measure each insect's dimensions. For example:
- length and width of body
- length of antennae
- length of legs
- length and width of head
- circumference of body.

How Heavy?
How do you measure the mass of a slater?
Weigh a number of them together and then divide the weight.

Art: Insect Symmetry

Fold a piece of drawing paper in half. Children draw half of an insect on one side, colouring thickly with wax crayon. Fold the paper over to cover the drawing. Cover the drawing paper with a sheet of newspaper and press with a warm iron. Unfold.

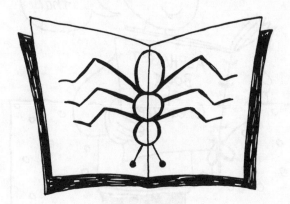

Blotting Paper Insects
Create ink blots on blotting paper. Children use ink blots to create their own fantasy creatures by adding:
- legs
- antennae
- wings
- eyes
- or whatever else they want to add.

Give it a name. Invent a profile for this new insect:
- habitat
- breeding habits
- food
- how it protects itself.

Cut out the blot insect and paste it onto a painting or a collage of the insect's environment.

Research: Insect Sense

Find out how insects hear, see and feel.

Eyes
Can you see its eyes?
How many are there?
Are they large or small?
Are they simple or compound eyes?
How does the shape and placement of eyes help the insect?
Does it prefer light or shade?

Ears
Can you find its ears?
How does it respond to loud noises?
What happens when you blow on the
insect?
What happens when you touch the
insect?

Wings
Does the insect have wings?
How many?
Are they the same size?
Are they clear, patterned, covered?

Legs
What are the legs used for?
How many sections does each leg
have?
Does the insect use its legs or its
wings more often?

Colours
What colour is the insect?
How many colours does it have?
How do you think the colour helps the
insect?
Can it change colours?

Movement
How does the insect move? Does it
walk, fly, hop, run, jump, crawl or
swim?
When it walks, how many legs stay on
the ground, how many are lifted?
Can it walk upside down?
Can it walk up the walls of its home?
When placed on its back, can it turn
itself the right way around quickly and
easily? Does it fly quickly or slowly,
for long distances or short distances?

Research: Insect Life Cycles

In groups or individually, children can
research:
- the life cycle of each insect collected
- each insect's relatives
- the food chain for each insect —
  what does the insect eat, and what
  eats this insect?
- useful insects and pests — which of
  the insects collected are useful, and
  which are pests?
- the sounds produced by insects, for
  example crickets and cicadas, and
  how the sounds are produced
- dangerous insects — which of the
  insects collected are harmful, and
  which are harmless?

Art: Make a Book

Make an alphabet book of creatures. All
information and artwork gathered from
previous activities can be entered in the
book.
  Making and keeping an alphabet book
of creatures can be a class, group or
individual activity.

Bees

Attracting Bees

Set up a small table with different types of food which the children think may attract bees.

Try different places in the school grounds to see which the bees prefer.

- How long did it take for the first bees to arrive?
- Did any other insects arrive?
- Did the bees come alone or in groups?
- Which food was the most popular?

Catch a bee using a transparent container or a glass jar with a lid.

In the classroom examine the bee (in the container). Look at its legs, eyes, mouth, wings, sting, segments, antennae and colours.

Return the bee to a safe place.

pipecleaners

cardboard cylinder

pipecleaners

Make a Model Bee

You will need:

- cardboard cylinder (10 cm long)
- pipecleaner for legs, antennae, sting and wings
- cellophane for wings
- yellow and black paper strips
- felt tipped pens

cellophane

Buzz Buzz Buzz

black and yellow paper strips

A Honey 'No Cooking' Recipe

Yummy Honey Balls

Ingredients

3 cups of raisins

3 cups of honey

3 cups of rice cereal (rice bubbles or puffed rice)

3 cups of peanut butter

1. Mix all the ingredients together and roll into balls.
2. Place balls on a tray and set in the fridge for about half an hour.

Honey

Find out about how honey is made. How is it harvested? How is it extracted from honeycomb?

Ants

Collect ants. It's not easy, but scoop them up quickly and put them in a plastic bag. Tie a knot in the top of the bag and place the bag in a cool place for a few hours. The ants will then be easier to put into the classroom habitat.

Feed the ants a drop of honey mixed with water, fruit, or hard boiled eggs. One drop of honey can feed fifty ants. Feed the ants a small quantity once a week. Ants need water so add a few drops of water to the soil each day or place a damp sponge on the surface of the soil.

Ant Experiments

These two experiments are about testing the ants' responses.
Outside, find some ants and create a trail of ants by placing a drop of sugary water nearby.

When the ant trail is well established, break the pathway by wiping across it with a wet finger. What happens? Why? (Ants are almost blind, they rely on the senses of touch and smell.)

When the trail has been re-established, have the children create shade and shadows above the ants. How do the ants react?

Now have the children thump the ground close to the trail. What happens? Why?

Ants and Bees

Ants and bees are social insects.
Find out about how they:
- structure their society
- communicate
- breed
- construct their homes
- protect their homes
- collect food.

Other social insects include wasps and termites.

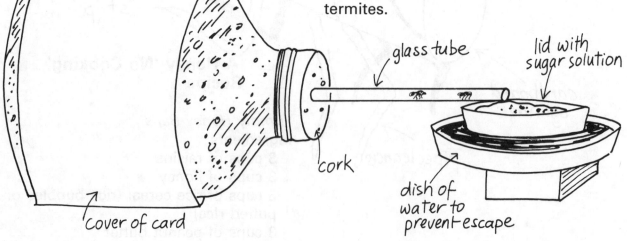

A classroom habitat for ants

glass tube

lid with sugar solution

cork

dish of water to prevent escape

cover of card

Art

Stained Glass Butterflies
Make 'stained glass butterflies', with black cardboard and coloured cellophane. Hang them in the classroom.

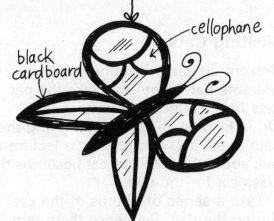

black cardboard

cellophane

Grow a Caterpillar
Cut six circles of decreasing sizes from *Chux* disposable cloths. Fill each with birdseed and tie with twist-tie to make varying sized balls. Make a face on the largest, and add pipe cleaner antennae. Arrange on a waterproof tray on a bed of damp cottonwool, and place on a sunny windowsill. Keep damp, and within a week the caterpillar should begin to sprout. Once in full growth, it should last about four or five weeks.

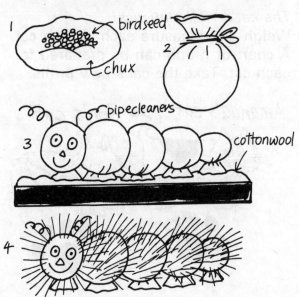

1   birdseed
     chux
2
3   pipecleaners   cottonwool
4

Egg Carton Insects
Use a small section of egg carton, add cellophane wings and pipe cleaner antennae to make butterflies or moths. Create imaginary insects from junk materials.

 Bibliography

Burton, Maurice, *Encyclopeadia of Insects and Arachnids*, Finsbury, 1984.

Carruth, Jane, *The Book of Fantastic Insects*, Octopus, 1975.

Clyne, Densey, *How to Keep Insects as Pets*, Angus and Robertson, 1978.

Cresswell, Helen, *The Beetle Hunt*, Longman, 1973

Dennis, C. J., *The Ant Explorer*, Macmillan, 1988.

Goldsmith, John, *It's Easy to have Ants to Stay*, Chatto and Windus, 1981.

Guth, Steven, *Honeybee*, Jacaranda, 1976.

Hughes, Jill, *Bees and Wasps*, Hamilton, 1976.

Ingves, Gunilla, *The Ant*, Hamilton, 1984.

Keneally, Thomas, *Ned Kelly and the City of the Bees,* Penguin, 1980.

Pinchin, Rebecca, *Insects*, Hodder and Stoughton, 1986.

Porter, Keith, *The Insect World,* The Animal Kingdom, Macmillan, London, 1986.

Steele, Mary, *Arkwright*, Hyland House, 1986.

Taylor, Lee, *The Insect Zoo and the Wildcat Hero,* Ashton Scholastic, 1985.

Williams, Kit, *Bees on the comb*, Cape, 1984.

Cats

Introducing Cats

Begin this theme by talking about 'famous' cats: for example, *Puss in Boots; Dick Whittington and his Cat;* Khat in *Midnite: the story of a wild colonial boy*, by Randolph Stow; Tom the cat from the cartoon, *Tom and Jerry;* and Sylvester the cat from the *Sylvester and Tweety Bird* cartoons.

Read the stories about these famous literary cats and about others from the bibliography.

Read *Old Possum's Book of Practical Cats* by T.S. Eliot. Play the songs from the Andrew Lloyd Webber musical, *Cats.*

Talk about the different personalities. Discuss how domestic cats show their 'personality'. How do these pet cats communicate with their owners?

Ask children to bring photos of their pet cats to school. Children display and write a brief personality profile for each picture.

Visiting Cats

Present an early morning cat show. (Parents participate and take the pet cats home after the show.)
Or, individual children could bring their cats to school, and present a lecture or talk about the cat. This cat becomes the class cat for the day.

Take a series of photos of the cat during the day. Sequence them and write about the cat's behaviour.

About the Cat's Visit
Write a story of the cat's visit:
- from the cat's viewpoint
- from the owner's viewpoint
- from the viewpoint of the class's budgerigar
- from the viewpoint of the mice that live behind the classroom cupboard
- from the teacher's point of view.

The cat's vital statistics!
Weigh and measure each visiting cat. A chart or graph can be prepared for each cat. Take the cat's paw prints.

Research: Cat Breeds

Find out about cat breeds. Classify them according to:

- shape
- length of fur
- markings
- colour
- size
- movement
- length of tail.

Siamese are my favourite breed!

Visiting Speaker

A Cat Breeder
Invite a cat breeder to class to talk about cats. Ask about:

- how cats breed
- the care the female cat gives to her kittens, and how she protects them
- the behaviour of a pregnant cat
- the early life of a kitten.

Member of a Cat Refuge or Cat Protection Group
Talk about:

- cats being dumped
- the need for feline birth control
- responsible pet ownership
- the problem of feral cats.

Class Discussion

Talk about:

- why do people keep cats as pets?
- how do owners look after their cats?
- what are the needs of the pet cat?

Survey

Cat products and accessories
Survey the range of cat foods to find out which is the most popular food.
Visit a pet shop to view the range. Discuss the cost of keeping a pet cat.

How much money is spent on cat food by a family that has one cat. How much money is spent on cat food by all the families with cats?

Cats or No Cats?
Not all people like cats.
Find out about their reasons for disliking cats.

Go away!

Class Debate

Debate the issue of cat ownership:
- responsibilities — what are the responsibilities of cat ownership?
- if the cat is not newted, who is responsible for the offspring?
- are owners responsible for what their cats kill, for example, native birds and wildlife?
- what happens to the family cat when the family goes away for a holiday?

Advertising Campaign

Plan an advertising campaign for 'responsible pet ownership'.
Make posters, write newspaper advertisements, record radio and video commercials.

Make Pet Ownership Buttons. Write slogans for the buttons.

 ## Research:
The History of Cats

Find out about the history of cat ownership. Find out about the importance of cats to:
- the Egyptians
- the Thais (Siamese cats).

Superstitions
Find out about cat superstitions. For example, black cats crossing one's path; cats and witches.

Sayings
Collect and record 'cat' sayings, for example:
- the cat's pyjamas
- the cat's whiskers
- the cat that got the cream
- raining cats and dogs
- letting the cat out of the bag
- looking like something the cat dragged in
- cat among the pigeons
- room to swing a cat.

Where did these sayings come from? Write stories to explain the origin of these sayings.

Poetry
Find poems about cats and read them. Write your own tanka poems. (A tanka is a Japanese poem of 31 syllables, arranged in 5 lines. The first and third lines have 5 syllables each, and the other have 7 syllables each.

For example:

Line 1	5 syllables
Line 2	7 syllables
Line 3	5 syllables
Line 4	7 syllables
Line 5	7 syllables

Use a felt-tipped pen to write the poems on balloons, and then display them.

Whiskas lives inside
He makes his home on the couch
Lazy and Tabby
He sprawls in the morning sun
And purrs when tickled by Mum.

Art

Cat Puppets
Make cat puppets using socks and material scraps.

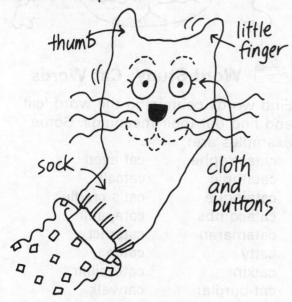

thumb

little finger

sock

cloth and buttons

Or make a cat puppet from a paper bag, straws and ruler.

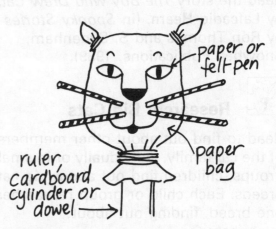

paper or felt pen

ruler, cardboard cylinder or dowel

paper bag

Cats from Basic Shapes
Use basic shapes to draw the head of a cat.
Use basic shapes to draw a seated cat.

1   2   3

1

2   3

27

Reading

Read the story *The Boy who Drew Cats* by Lafcadio Hearn, (in *Spooky Stories* by Ron Thomas and S. Sydenham, Snowball Publications, 1989).

 Research: Big Cats

Read to find out about other members of the cat family. Individually or in small groups, children find out about big cat breeds. Each child or group researches one breed, finding out about:

- appearance
- habitat
- food source (prey)
- protection behaviour
- breeding habits and life cycle
- life style
- enemies.

Results of research can be presented as:

- books — each group/child makes a book to present their research
- charts
- filmstrips
- dioramas
- and in any other way the child/group may choose.

Discussion: Big Cats

Discuss big cats in captivity:

- advantages/disadvantages of keeping big cats in zoos
- endangered species — how to protect them. Are zoos the best place to protect endangered species?

 Research: Prehistoric Cats

Find out about prehistoric cats, such as the sabre-toothed tiger.

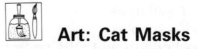 **Art: Cat Masks**

Make masks of cats. Masks can be of domestic cats, big cats and prehistoric cats. Use the information gathered in the previous activities about the features of cats to make the masks.

 Word Study: Cat Words

Find words containing the word 'cat' and find out their meanings. Some examples are:

catastrophe	cat-eyed
catatonic	catcall
catalogue	cat's cradle
catacombs	catapault
catamaran	cataract
catty	catch
catkin	caterpillar
cat-burglar	catwalk

Cat Dictionary

Make a cat dictionary. Find one word for each letter of the alphabet. Choose words that you think a cat would find interesting. For example:

m for mouse
d for dog
w for water
b for bowl
f for fish, and on.

Define each word from a cat's point of view. Illustrate each word.

MOUSE — a delicious crunchy fast food — Yum!

FISH — a swimming, swishing, smelly, tasty treat!

Bibliography

Anello, Christine, *The Farmyard Cat*, Ashton Scholastic, 1987.

Attmore, Stephen, *Now You can Read about Cats*, Brimax, 1984.

Butterworth, Christine, *Cats*, Macmillan 1988.

Castor, Harriet, *Fat Puss and Friends*, Penguin, 1985.

Coleridge, Ann, *Feral Animals,* Southern Cross, Macmillan, 1987.

Dick Whittington and his Cat, Traditional.

Eliot, T.S., *Old Possum's Book of Practical Cats*, Faber, 1975.

Feder, Jan, *The Life of a Cat*, Hutchinson, 1982.

Hearn, Lafcadio, *The Boy Who Drew Cats*, in Thomas and Sydenham *Spooky Stories*, Snowball Publications, 1988.

Kerr, Judith, *Mog and the Baby*, Mog Series, Collins, 1979.

Kerr, Judith, *Mog the Forgetful Cat*, Mog Series, Collins, 1979.

Martyr, Andrew, *Patch the Pirate Cat*, Hamilton; 1987.

Puss in Boots, Trad.

Smyth, Gwenda, *A Pet for Mrs. Arbuckle*, Ashton Scholastic, 1982.

Steeh, Judith A., *Cat Breeds*, Bison, 1984.

Stolz, Mary, *Cat Walk*, Collins, 1985.

Stow, Randolph, *Midnite*: the story of a wild colonial boy, Macmillan Books, 1986.

Clocks and Time

Introducing Clocks and Time

To begin this theme, ask each child to record one day's activities.
Children can record their day's activities on a circular chart that represents a clock face.

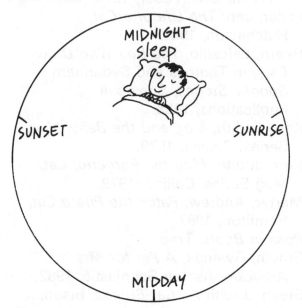

Or they can make a timeline.

Research: Clocks

Discuss ways of telling the time.
Collect clocks, or pictures of different types of clocks:
- sundials
- watches—different types, such as watch faces without numbers, digital watches, Mickey Mouse watches
- hourglass
- candle clocks
- water-clocks
- stopwatches
- parking meter clock
- automatic timing devices such as those on videos, ovens and security lights.

Science: Making Clocks

Make simplified versions of the clocks listed above.

Sundial
Make a simple sundial.
1. Push a stake into the ground and mark where the shadow falls.
2. Every hour, mark where the shadow falls.

Hourglass

Make a simple hourglass.

1. Make a small hole in the lid of a clean plastic bottle.
2. Cut the bottom off the bottle, and fill the bottle with fine sand.
3. Place the bottle into a clear jar. Paste a strip of paper on the side of the jar. On the strip of paper mark the level of sand at selected time intervals.

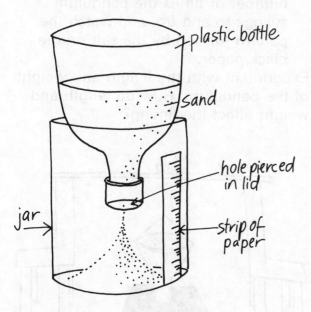

Candle Clock

Make a candle clock.

1. Stand a candle in some plasticene on a metal tray. Measure the candle.
2. Light the candle and let it burn for a selected interval, for example, ten minutes.
3. Blow out the candle and measure it. How much of the candle burnt in the time?
4. Mark another candle with lines the same distance apart, as measured on the first candle. Take note of the time when you light the candle, and you will be able to tell the time as the candle burns down to each line.

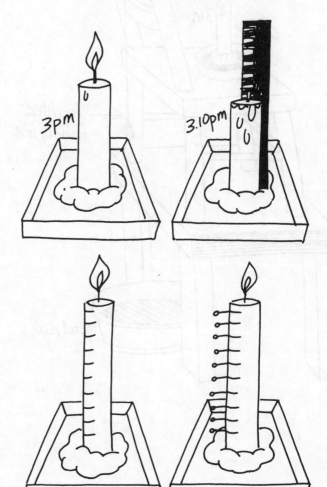

Waterclock

Make a simple waterclock.

1. Make a pinhole in the bottom of a paper cup.
2 Stand the cup in a clear jar. Paste a strip of paper onto the side of the jar.
3. Pour water into the cup. On the strip of paper, mark the level of water at selected time intervals.

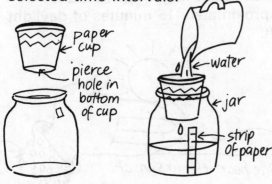

Candle Clock Alarm
Use your candle clock to make an alarm.
1. Insert a pin into the candle at the time you want the alarm to sound.
2. Attach a weighted fishing line to the pin, and hang the weight above a metal tray or baking dish.
3. When the candle burns down to the pin, the pin will be released and the weight will crash down onto the metal dish.

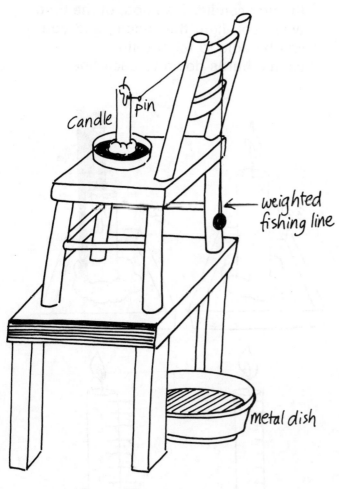

Pendulums
Make a pendulum.
1. Tie a length of string around the wide end of a funnel. Tie it so that when you hold the string vertically, the funnel sits upright.
2. Suspend the string and funnel vertically over a piece of black paper.
3. Fill the funnel with salt and set the pendulum in motion. Count the number of times the pendulum swings to and fro, and watch the pattern formed by the salt on the black paper.
Experiment with the length and weight of the pendulum. How do length and weight affect the timing?

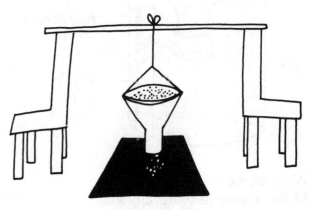

Tell the time by the sun
With arm outstretched, fill the space between the horizon and sun with your fingers (not the thumb), of one or both hands. Each finger represents approximately 15 minutes of daylight left.

One hour left to sunset

Research

Clock mechanics

Investigate the mechanical workings of clocks and watches. Collect some old clocks and watches to take apart. Or, observe the workings of a clock or watch with the back removed.

Telling Time in the Past

Collect books and read about the ways that people told the time in the past.

Record: How Long Does it Take?

In groups or pairs, children time and record how long it takes to do the following:

- run around the school buildings following a predetermined track
- write their name ten times
- bounce a ball twenty times
- eat lunch
- build a tower 1 metre tall
- 60 heartbeats.

Diaries

Keep a diary for one day. Write an entry every hour. Older children can keep a diary for a week.

Timelines

Children construct timelines of their lives marking significant events and dates.

My timeline

My school's timeline

Older children could make an illustrated timeline for their school. Individually or in groups, they could research significant events and dates in the school's history. Use old photos, newsletters and school records to illustrate the timeline.

Children can make timelines of other things such as:

- sporting heroes
- fashion
- cars
- film stars and pop stars
- world or a particular country's historical events
- a family history.

Class Discussion: Seasons

Talk about:
- the changes in the seasons
- the characteristics of each season
- what causes the changes
- activities particular to each season, such as sporting and leisure activities, types of food eaten and clothes worn, festivals, and animal behaviour.

Experiment: Timing Growth

Plant a bean seed or some cress seeds in a pot of soil in the class, or in your school garden. Graph the time taken for growth.

Word Study

Sayings About Time
Write down sayings about time.
For example:
- time flies
- having a good time
- the time of your life
- you're only young once
- racing against time
- old timer
- old man time
- the man in the moon
- time honoured
- to kill time
- to mark time
- taking time out
- serving time
- Eastern Standard Time
- time and time again
- once upon a time
- all in good time
- behind the times
- for the time being

- better late then never
- a stitch in time . . .
- the early bird gets the worm
- time waits for no-one
- slow coach
- all's well that ends well
- nothing lasts forever
- from time immemorial
- time stood still
- time on your hands
- time hangs heavy
- till death do us part

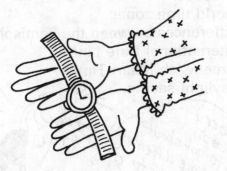

Words about Time

Make a list of words about time.
For example:

tempo	timely
speed	timesaving
fast	timetable
late	time sharing
tardy	time warp

Writing about Time

Use the following headings to write about time:

- advertise a season
- invent a fifth season
- when I was young
- in 20 years time.....
- the time machine

Make factual books about:

- the story of clocks
- how a clock works
- people of the past
- the life of an animal
- the people in the class — use baby photos to illustrate
- the history of the days of the week
- the months of the year.

Children can collect photographs from newspapers and magazines, and write about what had happened 5 minutes before or after the photo was taken.

Class Activity

Record a Day

Set up a camera on a tripod in a usually busy section of the yard. Take 1 photograph every 30 minutes to record the day's activities in that part of the yard. Begin early before school starts, and end late after school has finished. Use the photographs to make a timeline.

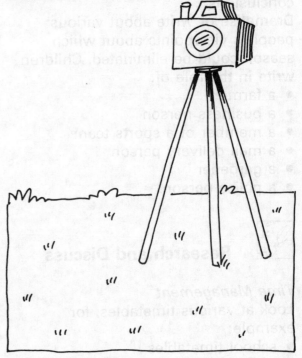

Timelapse Photography
Set up a video camera on a tripod to capture the movement of the clouds across the sky.

Operate the camera every half hour for 30 seconds throughout one day. The results are often best when shot on a windy or cloudy day.

Use timelapse photography to record the movement of trees, or traffic during one day.

Drama

Divide the class into groups of four. In each group, each child represents one of the seasons. They are told that one of the seasons is to be eliminated. Each 'season' must argue his or her case for being retained.

Group all the representatives of each season together. They have to prepare a case for their retention to present in a class debate against the other seasons.

After the debate and out of their roles, the class discusses the conclusions.

Dramatise or write about various people's viewpoints about which season could be eliminated. Children write in the role of:
- a farmer
- a business person
- a member of a sports team
- a mail delivery person
- a gardener
- a police person.

Research and Discuss

Time Management
Look at various timetables, for example:
- school timetables

- bus timetables
- train timetables
- aeroplane timetables
- shiftworker's timetable
- personal timetable.

Talk about:
- world time zones
- differences between the hemispheres
- International Date Line
- Greenwich Mean Time
- daylight-saving.

Talk about daytime and night-time:
- what happens in the community while we sleep?
- the people who work at night
- the activity of nocturnal animals
- the night sky
- the phases of the moon.

Music

Listen to 'As Time Goes By!'
'Time Warp' (from *The Rocky Horror Picture Show*), Festival Records, 1974.

Bibliography

Breiter, Herta S., *Time and Clocks*, Raintree, 1978.

Christensen, Nadia, *The Magic Clock*, Warne, 1979.

Clarke, Jenny, *The Grass that Grew*, Southern Cross, Macmillan, 1989.

Hutchins, Pat, *Clocks and more Clocks*, Bodley Head, 1970.

Jennings, Terry, *Time*, Oxford University Press, 1988.

Kirst, Werner, *Time*, Hart-Davis, 1977.

Krasilovsky, Phyllis, *The Man who tried to Save Time*, Doubleday, 1979.

Mitchell, Greg, *Six Seasons*, Southern Cross, Macmillan, 1987.

Odgers, Sally Farrell, *Hey Mum!*, Southern Cross, Macmillan, 1989.

Robertson, Robin, *It's About Time: A History of Clocks and Calendars*, Southern Cross, Macmillan, 1987.

Thomas, Ron and Stutchbury, Jan, *Autumn*, Macmillan Beginners, Macmillan, 1987.

Thomas, Ron and Stutchbury, Jan, *Clocks and Watches*, Macmillan Beginners, Macmillan, 1989.

Thomas, Ron and Stutchbury, Jan, *Spring*, Macmillan Beginners, Macmillan, 1989.

Thomas, Ron and Stutchbury, Jan, *Summer*, Macmillan Beginners, Macmillan, 1987.

Thomas, Ron and Stutchbury, Jan, *Winter*, Macmillan Beginners, Macmillan, 1987.

What's the Time, Mr Wolf?, Southern Cross, Macmillan, 1987.

Dinosaurs

Introducing Dinosaurs

Make a calligraphy dinosaur.

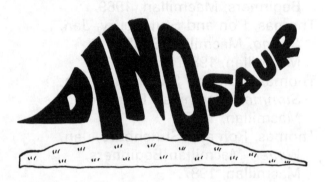

Research: Dinosaur Size

Using a metre rule, measure out the length (21 metres) of an *Apatosaurus*, which is one of the sauropods.

Cut a piece of string the same length and go on a hunt for things the same size as the *Apatosaurus.*

On a grid 9 metres wide and 4 metres deep marked out 1 metre squares. Draw the dinosaur as shown.
How many people will fit inside the dinosaur? How long does it take you to:
- walk around the shape?
- hop around the shape?
- bounce a ball around the shape?

Scale Drawing
Older children could repeat the drawing of the dinosaur on the scale of 1 centimetre: 1 metre.
On grid paper they will be able to determine the area.

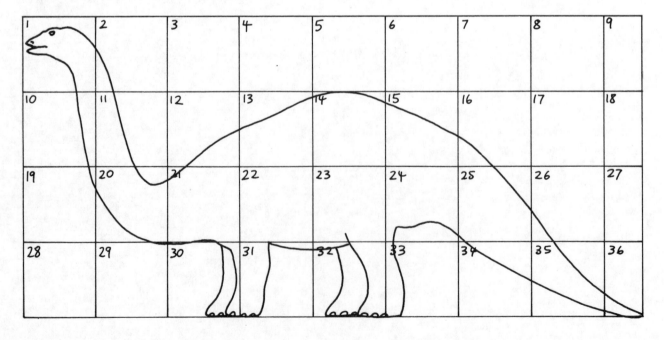

Research: Dinosaurs

Find out about:
- the times when the various dinosaurs lived
- the theories about why the dinosaurs became extinct.

Classify dinosaurs into groups such as:
- plant eaters
- meat eaters
- flying dinosaurs
- aquatic dinosaurs and so on.

Art: Model Dinosaurs

Make papier-mache or clay models of the various dinosaurs. Build an appropriate environment for the models.

Make dinosaur footprints. Measure out and draw the shape of a dinosaur's footprint based on the knowledge (acquired in previous activities) of dinosaur dimensions. Mould the footprint in damp sand.
Make a plaster cast.

Writing: Dinosaur Cartoons

Write a cartoon story about finding a dinosaur.
Discuss and resolve the problems of dinosaur ownership.

Mapping
Read *Thing* by Robin Klein and *The Village Dinosaur* by Phyllis Arkle (see *Bibliography*).

Use these stories to make maps of the settings in which the events in the stories take place.

Plan a daily routine for the care and feeding of a dinosaur in captivity.
- What are its food requirements?
- How much food will be needed?
- Where will the food come from?
- How much will the food cost?
- How will you offset the costs?
- What will you charge people to see the dinosaur?

- How many people will you need to visit the dinosaur each day to pay for the dinosaur's daily food costs?
- Who will clean out the dinosaur's shed or living area?
- Can you sell the manure?
- Does the dinosaur need daily exercise?

 Game: Concentration

Make a concentration card game using enlarged photocopied outlines as shown.

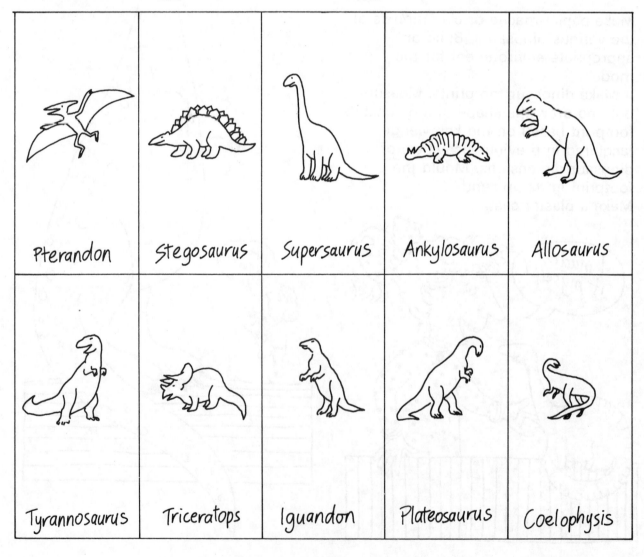

| Pterandon | Stegosaurus | Supersaurus | Ankylosaurus | Allosaurus |
| Tyrannosaurus | Triceratops | Iguandon | Plateosaurus | Coelophysis |

Bibliography

Anderson, Jan, *The Days of the Dinosaurs*, Nelson, 1985.

Arkle, Phyllis, *The Village Dinosaur*, Penguin, 1979.

Asimov, Isaac, *Did Comets Kill the Dinosaurs?*, Collins, 1985.

Australian Dinosaurs and their World, Golden Press, Sydney, 1987.

Breidahl, Harry, *Gifts from Gondwanaland,* Southern Cross, Macmillan, 1987.

Cox, Barry, *Collins illustrated Encyclopaedia of Dinosaurs and Prehistoric Creatures*, Collins, 1988.

Keen, Martin L., *Dinosaurs*, Grosset and Dunlap, 1982.

Kingdon, Jill, *The ABC Dinosaur Book*, Children's Press, 1982.

Klein, Robin, *Thing*, OUP, 1982.

Klein, Robin, *Thingnapped*, OUP, 1984.

Lambert, David, *Collins Guide to Dinosaurs*, William Collins, 1983.

Lambert, David, *Dinosaur World*, Pan, 1981.

LaPlaca, Michael, *How to draw Dinosaurs*, Watermill, 1982.

Oliver, Rupert, *Dinosaurs*, Hodder and Stoughton, 1983.

Orr, Wendy, *Amanda's Dinosaur*, Ashton Scholastic, 1988.

Richler, Mordecai, *Jacob two-two and the Dinosaur*, McClellands and Stewart, 1987.

Sydenham, Shirley, *Dinosaurs,* Macmillan Black Line Masters, Macmillan, 1989.

Thomas, Ron and Stutchbury, Jan, *Dinosaurs,* Macmillan Beginners, Macmillan, 1988.

Dragons

Introducing Dragons

Begin this theme by reading lots of stories about dragons. Discuss the various kinds of dragons, such as:

- cruel and wicked dragons
- kind and wise dragons
- bringers of good fortune
- misunderstood dragons
- devourers of maidens.

Story Retellings
Try story retellings:

- as comic strip stories
- wall frieze of events
- orally onto tape as a radio play with sound effects
- group retelling ground a circle.

Read *The Dragon in the Clock Box* by Jean M. Craig (see *Bibliography*). After reading, draw and label the life cycle of a dragon.

Make a timeline of the dragon's incubation, hatching, wing growing, tailgrowing and so on.

← Incubation →   Hatching

0	1 YEAR

First tooth	Wings start to grow	Wings fully grown
14 MONTHS	18 MONTHS	2 YEARS

Tail fully grown	First solo flight
25 MONTHS	26 MONTHS

First damsel devoured	First prince fought
28 MONTHS	30 MONTHS

Newspaper headlines
Make fliers for each of the dragon stories.

Word Study: Dragon Words

List words that tell about dragons. Which words tell about:
- what they look like?
- how they move?
- what sounds they make?
- what they feel like?
- what they eat?
- where they live?
- what they do?

Use these words to create your own dragon. Tell someone about your dragon.

Invent the life history of your dragon, and draw its family tree. Make a dragon family photo album.

Write about one of your dragon's adventures. Draw or paint pictures to illustrate your story.

Pet Dragons

Talk about keeping a dragon as a pet:
- What are its needs?
- Where do you keep it?
- Where does it sleep?
- What will you feed it?
- How do you exercise it?
- How do you bath it?
- What will you call it?
- Where did you find it?

Make a model of the pet dragon and look after it in the classroom.

Write about the day you took your pet dragon to the vet.
- What was wrong with it?
- How did you get it there?
- What was the reaction of the other pet owners and of their pets in the waiting room?
- How did the vet examine your dragon?
- What was the treatment prescribed?

Write about:
- the day you entered your pet dragon in the local pet show.
- The day your pet dragon followed you to school. What was the reaction of that teacher you don't like?
- A day at the beach with your pet dragon.

Dragon Acrostic

Dragon
Roaring
Angry
Grazing
On
Nettles

Pet Dragon Show
Hold a pet dragon show. Invent suitable prizes for the owners of pet dragons.

Game

Dragon-by-the-Tail

Players line up one behind the other grasping the waist of the person in front. The person at the front of the dragon has to try to touch the person at the end of the tail, dragging the dragon as he or she tries to do so. Anyone who lets go is out of the game.

When the person at the front succeeds in touching the person at the end, he or she goes to the end of the line and the next person becomes the head.

Dragon Tiggy

When a person is tagged by 'he', the two join hands and so on until all players are joined to form one long dragon.

Dragon Board Game

Make a board game to follow the sequence of a favourite dragon story.
Or, make a 'dragons and ladders' game.

Or, make a trail game to find the dragon's treasure.
Or, make up a variation of Battleship.

6 across 2 down...

Dragon Pros and Cons

Think about the good and bad aspects of owning a dragon. For example:
I have a dragon who keeps the house warm, that's good...
but we can't turn him off in the summer, that's bad...
but we have great barbeques, that's good....
but he sometimes burns the meat, that's bad......
and so on.

Art

Dragon Mural

Make a class mural of dragons. It can be a long scene with lots of dragon activity.

Or it can be one long dragon collage. Use a variety of materials to make the dragon tactile.

Dragon Model
Use clay to make models of dragons. Build an environment for the dragon models. Tape-record sound effects.

Stick Puppet
Make a long stick puppet of a dragon to be operated by 3 or 4 children. The dragon's head can be made from papier-mache, or it can be a painted balloon, or it can be made from cardboard and decorated with paints or material.

The body can be made from one long piece of material, or from different pieces sewn together. Attach the head to the body, and attach the sticks at equal intervals as illustrated.

Sock Puppet
Make a sock puppet of a dragon. Sew spangled triangles and sequins onto the sock for scales. Attach bright pieces of material to the mouth for flames.

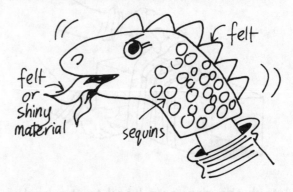

Chinese New Year Dragon
Make a Chinese New Year Dragon using a milk carton and some brightly coloured streamers, threads, ribbons and paper. First, make a dragon's head, as illustrated. Colour it in, cut it out and fold in half.

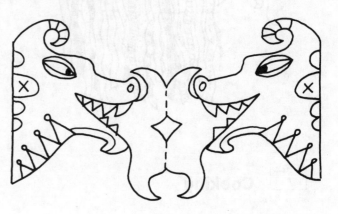

Then, cut off the top and bottom of the milk carton to make a dragon's body. (X marks the place for paper fasteners).

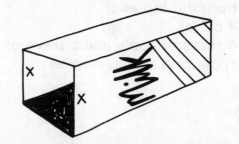

Wrap coloured paper around the outside of the carton. Staple long streamers of wool and coloured paper along the spine.

Attach the dragon's head to the body with paper fasteners (where marked X).

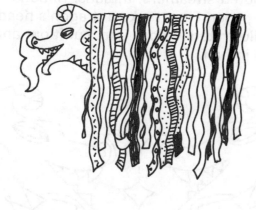

Cooking

Ca-bana the Dragon
Ingredients
1 piece of cabana (about 12cm long)
1 cheese 'single'
1 cheese wedge or triangle
4 stuffed olives
carrot — pointy tip (about 2cm long)
1 celery stick (about 6cm long and cut from the top end)
4 cloves
4 slices of apple and a piece of red apple peel, cut in a spiral

Things you will need:
Toothpicks for joining the pieces together
Knife
Vegetable peeler

1. Cut a groove along the length of the cabana, so that the triangles cut from the cheese 'single' will stand up along the dragon's back.
2. Cut a wedge of cheese for the head.
3. Cut the apple slices into clawed foot shapes.
4. Cut 4 triangles from the cheese 'single' — 3 for the back and one for the end of the tail.
5. Using toothpicks to join the pieces together, assemble the dragon as shown in the illustration below.

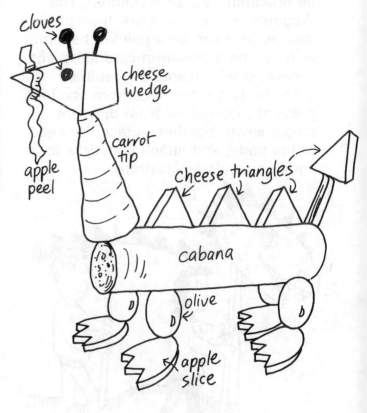

Word Study

Invent a word dragon. Make a list of dragon words such as:

scales	green	smoke
flames	claws	winged
fiery	dangerous	roaring
fierce	wise	snorting

Use your dragon words to draw a word dragon.

In small groups children prepare a television news item reporting sightings of dragons in the locality.

Drama

Warm-up by playing Dragon's Treasure. The dragon stands at one end of the room with back to the class. The rest of the class are grouped at the other end of the room. The treasure (such as a bean bag) is placed on the floor behind the dragon.

The class sneak forward and try to snatch the treasure. When the dragon turns around, everyone must freeze. If the dragon sees anyone moving, that person must return to the start.

If anyone succeeds in snatching the treasure, the dragon tries to tag them before they reach home (i.e. the start).

Children, in pairs, are designated A and B. A is a dragon and B is someone who is studying about dragons and who has at last met one. They improvise a conversation.

Talk about dragons and share the information that was discovered in the previous activity.

Divide the class into two groups: one group is a family of dragons who have lived at the top of a mountain for several centuries. The other group is the population of the town which has grown up at the bottom of the mountain. The townspeople want the dragons to move.

Give the groups some time for discussion. The dragons have to work out details of their lifestyle, their view of their importance to the townspeople, and why they should stay put.

The townspeople need to decide why they want the dragons to move and how they are going to acheive this. All children in both groups need to establish their roles.

Bring the groups together for an initial meeting to discuss the situation. Allow time for the meeting to develop before separating the groups.

After the initial meeting, each group discusses what has taken place and plans a strategy for the next meeting.

Hold the second meeting. After the second meeting, hold a class post-mortem to discuss the issues raised.

Drama Follow Up
Be a reporter. Write a newspaper or television report about the meetings held in the previous activity. Interview participants and record on audio or video tapes.

Use a computer package such as 'Newsroom' to design the front page of the newspaper reporting the series of meetings.

Art

A Dragon Parade
Organise a school dragon parade. Each class makes a dragon using cardboard boxes.

Or, you can use lengths of material.

Writing: Dragon Rhymes

Write a dragon rhyme. List words that rhyme with dragon and use them to construct dragon rhymes.

Use the rhyming dragon words to make up:
- a chant for scaring away dragons
- a rhyme for counting people to see who will be 'he' in a game
- a rhyme for a skipping game.

Take a Dragon for a Walk
Enlarge the pattern for a walking
dragon using an overhead projector.
Duplicate one for each child.
   Assemble using split pin paper
fasteners. Cover the dragon with pieces
of coloured paper, foil or Easter egg
wrapping.

Bibliography

Cas, Joan, *A Book of Dragons*, Arrow,
   1988.
Computer Software, *Dragon World*,
   BBC.
Craig, M. Jean, *The Dragon in the Clock
   Box*, Worlds Work, 1984.
Heck, Elisabeth, *The Young Dragon*,
   Burke, 1985.
Klein, Robin, *Brock and the Dragon*,
   Hodder and Stoughton, 1984.
Mahy, Margaret, *The Dragon of an
   Ordinary Family*, Heinemann, 1969.
Peet, Bill, *How Droofus the Dragon lost
   his Head*, Deutsch, 1985.
Scullard, Sue, *Miss Fanshawe and the
   Great Dragon,* Macmillan, 1986.
Willis, Val, *The Secret in the Matchbox*,
   Deutsch, 1988.

Earthworms

Introducing Earthworms

To begin this theme, make a wormery in the classroom, ready for a collection of worms.

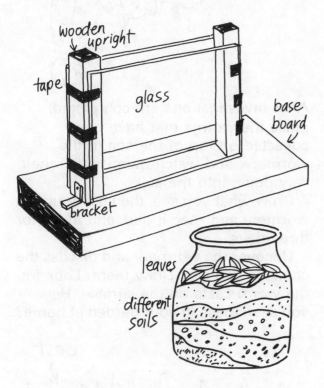

Fill the wormery with layers of contrasting coloured soil, sand and compost. Cover the top with dead leaves. Keep the contents moist but not too wet, or you'll drown the worms.

If you make the wormery narrow and keep it dark, (i.e. only uncovering to observe for short intervals), the worms may mate and produce eggs, and may be observed doing so.

Worm Hunt

Go on a worm hunt. Dig carefully in cool, moist soil. Or after a rainfall, you may find them on the surface, which makes them easier to collect.

Pose the question: why are earthworms found on the surface after a rainfall?

Examining Worms

Let the earthworms crawl on your hands, and talk about what it feels like. Rub a finger gently along the underside. What can you feel? What colour is the worm? Why are worms moist and slimy?

Look at a worm through a magnifying glass. What do you think the small bristles on the lower half of the worm's body are for?

Observe the rings and the saddle. How many rings does it have? Do small worms have as many rings as big worms? Find out the purpose of the saddle or girdle.

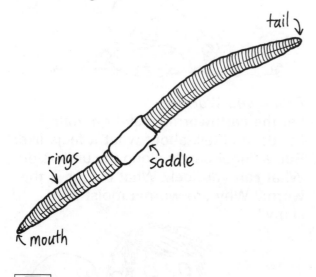

 Experiment

Can Worms Swim?
Place a large worm into slightly warmed (tepid) water for a few moments. Observe its behaviour. Look for the worm's mouth. Does it have ears? Does it have eyes?

Find the black line running along the worm from its head to its tail. What do you think it is?

The black line looks like a seam...

After investigations are completed, place the worms that have been collected on top of the soil in the wormery, and watch them tunnel their way down into the soil.

Draw what you see, then cover up the wormery and keep it dark and moist for three days.

Uncover the wormery and discuss the changes you see. Draw them. Look for the worm casts on the surface. Have you seen these in your garden at home?

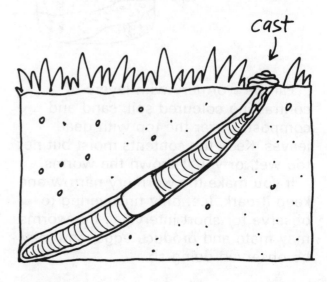

Research: About Worms

Children research to find out about the following questions.

- Do worms have lungs and a heart?
- How do they breathe under the ground?
- Are they helpful? If so, in what way?
- What happens if the ground gets too wet? Too dry?
- What are the worms enemies?
- How long do worms live for?
- Do worms have skeletons?

The Worm's Relatives

Find out about the giant earthworms in Gippsland, Victoria. What other worms can you find out about?

When you have finished with your earthworms, return them to a hole in the garden.

Bibliography

Aston, Oliver, *Earthworms*, Blackwell, 1977.

Jennings, Larry, *Earthworms*, OUP, 1988.

Pigdon, Keith and Woolley, Marilyn, *Earthworms*, Southern Cross, Macmillan, 1989. (Big Book and Reader)

Rockwell, Thomas, *How to eat Fried Worms*, Pan Books, 1979.

Eggs: a flow chart

Introduction: About Eggs

Discuss the egg as a symbol of new life, and the significance to Christians, and to the Europeans.

Other Egg Laying Animals
Find out about other animals that lay eggs. How are the eggs different? Where are they laid? How long do they take to hatch? How many are laid at a time?

Study the life cycles of animals that lay eggs, for example, spiders, crocodiles, frogs and lizards. Find out which reptiles, insects and amphibians lay eggs. Find out about dinosaurs' eggs. (A fossilised dinosaur egg was once found.)

Debate: Free-range v Battery Eggs

Find out the difference between free-range and battery eggs.

Games

Run:
- egg and spoon races
- roll the egg relay races.

Monotremes
Study monotremes, such as the platypus and echidnas. Their egg laying is of interest because they are mammals, and after hatching, the young are fed on milk.

Class Discussion: Human Eggs

Talk about the egg in human reproduction.

Art: Decorate Eggs

Decorate eggs. Dye them with food dye. Paint them with acrylic paints. Draw patterns on the eggs using felt-tipped pens. Decorate the eggs by pasting on scraps of material, sequins and anything else you fancy.

If hard-boiled eggs aren't used, you will need to blow the filling out of the eggs. Use a pin to make a hole at each end of the egg. Blow into one end and the egg will pour out the other.

Experiment: Hatching Eggs

Hatch some eggs in an incubator you have hired. Chickens are then kept in a brooder. Research the stages of the chick's development inside the egg. Give each child one egg so that when the eggs hatch, each chick will imprint with one child.

Crack open an egg bought from a shop. Study the parts. Find out about each part. Notice the sac left in the shell.

Other things to research:
- How does the developing embryo breathe?
- How does carbon dioxide escape? (The egg shell is porous, and this can be seen with a magnifying glass.)
- What is the shell made of?

Experiment: Test the Strength of Eggs

Take estimations from the class before the experiment. Is the strength of a free-range egg greater or less than a battery hen's egg?

Weigh eggs. Compare the weights of raw eggs and hard-boiled eggs, and eggs of different sizes.

Cook eggs in different ways. Survey children and other people (such as parents and family members) about their favourite way of eating eggs.

Find out about the nutritional value of an egg. Find out about foods that contain eggs.

Research

Make a classification of the various shapes and sizes of birds' eggs. Find out what you call a person who studies birds' eggs. (Oologist)

Which bird lays the smallest/largest egg? How are the eggs protected by the parent bird? How does the colour of the egg protect it? Find out about:
- the nesting habits of various birds
- the role of the male/female in the brooding/rearing of the young.

Bibliography

Chapman, Jean, *Pancakes and Painted Eggs*, Hodder and Stoughton, 1981.

Heller, Ruth, *Chickens aren't the only ones*, Grosset and Dunlap, 1981.

Hinds, Lorna, *Eggs*, Watts, 1975.

Pigdon, Keith and Woolley, Marilyn, *Incubation,* Southern Cross, Macmillan, 1989.

Polacco, Patricia, *Rechenka's eggs*, Collins, 1988.

Rodger, Sandi and Williams, Lyn, *The Easter Write Centre,* Macmillan Black Line Masters, Macmillan, 1989.

The Chicken and the Egg, Reed, 1979.

Flying Things

Introducing Flying Things

To begin this theme read one of the stories from the bibliography.

Or, show a video involving a flight, such as *The Red Balloon* or *The Boy Who Could Fly*.

Word Study

List all the things that the children can think of about flight, and classify under:

- animals that fly
- machines that fly
- people that fly
- insects
- plants
- flight in fantasy, such as 'Peter Pan' and 'Chitty Chitty Bang Bang', or other headings suggested by the children.

Art: Making Things That Fly

Paper Planes
Make a simple paper plane.

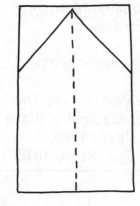
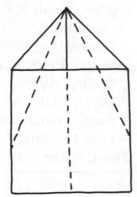

Make a flying tiger.

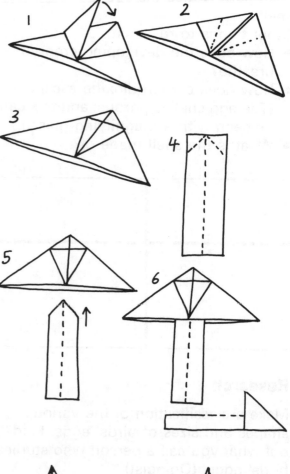

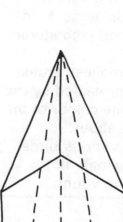
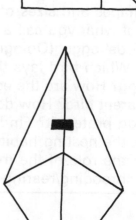

Make a whirlybird.
1. Cut along the solid lines.
2. Lines 1, 2 and 3: fold forward.
   Line 4: fold backward.
3. Decorate with different colours.
4. Hold your whirlybird up high and let it drop.

4. After decorating with scales, lightly stuff the fish with paper.
5. Make a ring from the wire. Fold and paste the mouth end of the fish over the wire. Then attach the string. The carp kite can also be made from thin fabric. Decorate with fabric crayons. Make a huge carp kite for the school flag pole.

Carp Kites
Make a carp kite.
You will need:
   wrapping paper
   thin wire
   glue
   crayons
   string
   scissors
1. Draw a fish shape. Copy it so you have two copies.
2. Join the two halves together by gluing the edges only.
3. Decorate your fish with scales. Use different coloured papers to make the scales. Start pasting on scales from the tail end of the fish.

Traditional Kite
Make a traditional kite.
You will need:
   4 sticks
   twine
   wrapping paper
   glue
   string
   rags and crepe paper

1. Position the sticks as illustrated and use the twine to tie them together to make a frame for the kite.

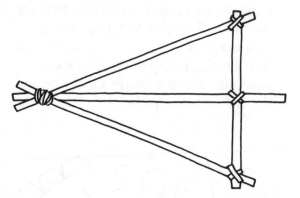

2. Cut a triangle from the wrapping paper, about 5 cm bigger than the frame on each side. Place the frame on the paper.

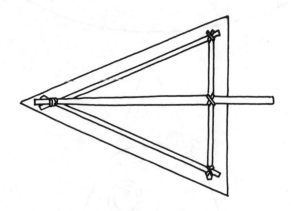

3. Glue the paper to the frame.

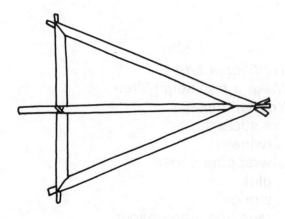

4. Make a bridle as illustrated, and wind the flying string onto a stick.
5. Make a tail for the kite. Tie strips of rags or crepe paper to a length of string at regular intervals. Attach the tail to the base of the kite.

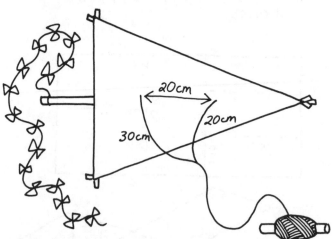

Experiment with kite making.
Can the children make a kite in the shape of those things on their original lists, for example, a kite in the shape of a bird, insect, Peter Pan, pterodactyl?

A Parachute
Make a parachute for the time when your flying machine fails to work.
You will need a square of lightweight fabric, string and scissors.

Research: Things that Fly

Find out about the following topics.
- The history of aviation — and before the Wright Brothers.
- Zeppelins and air ships.
- Helicopters.
- Early aviators.
- Prehistoric animals that could fly, such as the pterosaur.
- The principles of flight.
- Space flight
- Supersonic aircraft today and in the future.

Birds

Find out about birds:
- the largest and the fastest
- how the wings work
- the difference in wing shape
- flightless birds.

Investigate feathers:
- What holds the parts together?
- How many different sizes and shapes can you collect?
- What kind floats best?

Try constructing an artificial feather.

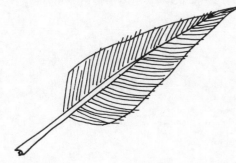

Insects

Find out about flying insects:
- wing shapes and structure
- insects with one pair and two pairs of wings
- insects that have wings for only a part of their lives.

Things That Fly Without Engines

Find out about things that fly without engines:
- gliders
- hang-gliders
- hot-air balloons.

Experiment With Balloons

Stretch the opening of a balloon over the neck of clean glass bottle. Stand the bottle in a saucepan containing about 5 centimetres of water. Place the saucepan on a low heat. What happens? (Hot air rises and lifts the balloon.)

Balloon Messages
Launch helium filled balloons with messages attached so that the people who find them can write back saying where the balloon was found. Mark on a map the location of the found balloons.

Weather Balloons
Find out about the use of balloons in weather forecasting.

Visiting Speakers

Arrange for the following people to come and speak to the class:
- a meteorologist
- a hot-air balloonist
- a pilot
- a glider pilot
- a person who hang-glides
- air traffic controller.

Excursions

Arrange class excursions to:
- the airport
- the museum
- a heliport
- the zoo.

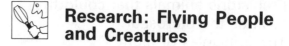

Research: Flying People and Creatures

Read about people who flew and winged creatures, such as:
- Hermes
- Icarus
- Pegasus
- Dragons
- Witches
- Angels
- Superman
- Mary Poppins
- Peter Pan
- Mother Goose

Retell these stories in Big Book format for group reading. Prepare scripts for radio plays. Make matchbox movies.

Art

Bird's-eye View

Look at aerial photographs and pictures taken from planes and spacecraft.
Draw and paint scenes and views of things and places as seen from above.

Mobiles

Design mobiles with a flight theme.
Children can make mobiles of:

- insects
- birds
- spacecraft
- witches.

Curly Birds

Make a curly bird.
Curl paper strips around pencils, rulers, matchsticks to make the curled paper necessary for the construction.

A collection of curly birds could be arranged in a model aviary.

Models

Invent and build a flying machine. Create a story or series of adventures for the flying machine and those who fly in it.

This could be published as a picture story book or as a cartoon strip.

 Writing Starters

- The day the cat flew.
- My mum grew wings.
- A ride on Pegasus.
- The Balloon's Escape!
- Log Book of Mars Probe 4.
- Invent a Service Manual for a witch's broom.
- An advertising brochure for a 'Build Your Own Wings' kit.

Science

Blowing Bubbles
Bubbles fly!
Make a solution of detergent and water (add some glycerine to make stronger, glossier bubbles).

Blow the bubbles outside on a breezy day. Discuss the colours and how the bubbles move. Bend a wire coat-hanger into a large loop, and fill a bucket with soapy solution. Wave the soapy coat-hanger to release the bubbles.
Make your own bubble wands by bending copper wire (or any easily bendable wire) into different shapes, as illustrated. Make sure they are all closed shapes to enable a bubble to form.
What effect do the different wire shapes have on the shape of the bubbles and their ability to 'fly'?

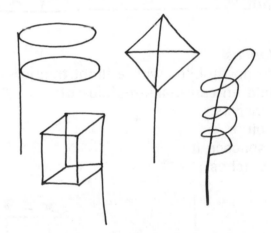

Make a Windvane
Discuss the importance of wind and its effects on flight.

Make a windvane. Cut out a large arrow from a piece of stiff cardboard. Sticky tape a small weight such as a washer or metal nut onto the point of the arrow. By inserting a pin and suspending the arrow, find the point where the arrow balances, and make a hole at that point. Tie string through the hole and hang the arrow in a spot that catches the wind.

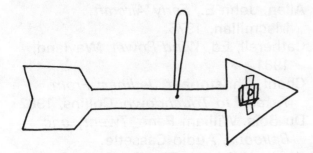

![magnifier icon] **Research: Flying Seeds**

List all the plants that use the wind to disperse their seeds. Find as many as you can and examine their structure to see how the wind is caught and utilised.

![face icon] **Drama: Going on a Flight**

You are passengers on the first Mars flight via the moon. Children will need to design and make:
- passports
- tickets
- boarding passes

They will need to decide what luggage they will need to take, and what they will be allowed to take. What security checks will be necessary?

In-flight, they will need to:
- design flight crew uniforms
- decide on tasks
- write menus for in-flight meals
- plan in-flight entertainment

A one-day overnight stopover on the moon will include a four hour sight-seeing tour:
- plan it
- draw the photos that would have been taken.

Continue the flight to its destination, with similar activities.
Role play the various situations that occur at airports and in-flight:
- checking in baggage
- security checks
- seat allocation
- general busy activities.

Then, flight station announcement: 'Ladies and gentlemen, Flight 2 to Mars via the moon has been delayed for five hours'. Children react in role.

More in-flight events
- act out the delivering of safety instructions (children can devise what they think is applicable for space travel).

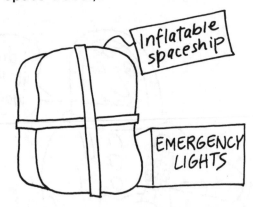

Passengers in the craft face a crisis:
- meteor shower
- problems in the approach to moon orbit
- hijacker.

How do they solve these crisis? Children respond in roles they have created as passengers.

After the crisis, reporters on the flight must relay a news broadcast to earth. Children write in role, the viewpoint of:
- an old lady
- a blind passenger
- a child
- a news reporter
- a pilot
- inflight crew.

Bibliography

Airliners, Trocadero, 1985.

Allen, John E., *Early Aircraft*, Macmillan, 1976.

Catherell, Ed, *Wind Power,* Wayland, 1981.

Chant, Christopher, *Jetliner: From Takeoff to Touchdown*, Collins, 1982.

Du Bois, William Pene, *Twenty-one Balloons*, Audio Cassette.

Dugan, Michael, *The Teacher's Secret*, Penguin, 1986.

Dyson, John, *Fun with kites*, Angus and Robertson, 1987.

Hughes, Shirley, *Up and Up*, Bodley Head, 1979.

Lamorisse, Albert, *The Red Balloon*, Allen and Unwin, 1980.

Newnham, Jack, *Kites to Make and Fly*, Penguin, 1977.

Nicklaus, Carol, *Flying, Gliding and Whirling*, Watts, 1981.

Paulsen, Gary, *Launching, Floating High and Landing*, Raintree.

Pick, Christopher, *Aircraft*, Galley, 1979.

Frogs

Introducing Frogs

Begin this theme by:
- reading stories about frogs (see *Bibliography*)
- studying a chart of the life cycle of a frog
- observing live frogs and tadpoles.

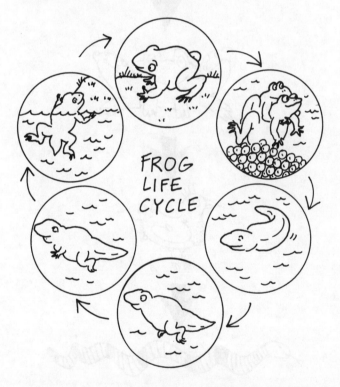

FROG LIFE CYCLE

Find out about different species of frogs:
- habits
- habitats
- adaptations to specific environments
- food requirements
- movement
- defensive behaviour.

Find out where different frogs come from, (i.e. country of origin).
Find out the names of different frogs, and where the names came from, for example, bull frogs and tree frogs.

Writing: Make a Book

Write descriptions of frogs based on your research. Make your own information books.

Science: frog habitat

If you have a frog in the classroom, create an appropriate environment.

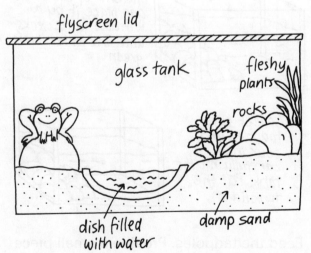

flyscreen lid

glass tank

fleshy plants

rocks

dish filled with water

damp sand

Observe and experiment with your class frog to find out about the following.

- How does it react to touch, sound and light?
- What does it feel like?
- How far can it jump?
- What happens when you kiss it?
- How much food does it eat?
- How does it catch food?

Tadpoles
If you are keeping tadpoles, create an appropriate environment.

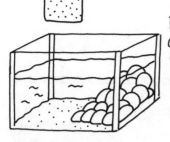

Put water in a glass tank

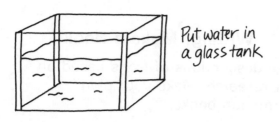

Wash a beaker of sand and spread the sand at the bottom of the tank

Pile some rocks at one end of the tank and place it by a window for 2 weeks until the water turns green.

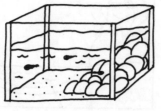

Collect some tadpoles and pour them carefully into the tank. Put the tank lid on.

Feed the tadpoles. Provide a small piece of boiled lettuce. (Boiling the lettuce makes it soft). Or, feed the tadpoles a pinch of Farex (baby food).

 Research

Make charts about frogs to show:

- labelled parts of a frog
- life cycle
- identification chart of frogs
- frogs of the world illustrated on a map
- food chains involving frogs.

Other Amphibians
Find out about other amphibians and make similar charts about them. (Other amphibians include toads, newts, salamanders, and axolotls).

Writing

Write a frog acrostic or cinquain.

Funny frogs
Rock n' Roll
Over
Green grass

_____(describes it)
_____ _____ _____ (describes movement)
_____ _____ _____ _____ (describes feelings)
_____ (synonym)

Make a poetry badge to display your frog acrostic or cinquain.

1. Cut out a cardboard circle (about 8 centimetres in diameter), or use an old badge.
2. Cover the cardboard circle or an old badge with a slightly bigger circle of coloured paper.
3. Make cuts as shown.
4. Fold edges over and tape.
5. Attach a safety pin with cellotape.

Write a poem on the front.

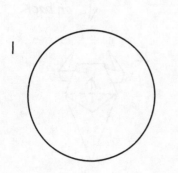

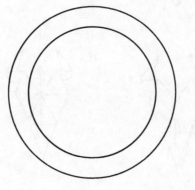

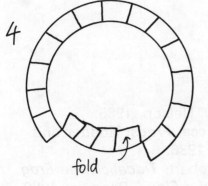

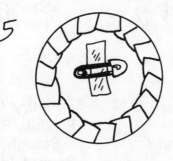

Art: Origami frog

Make an origami frog.

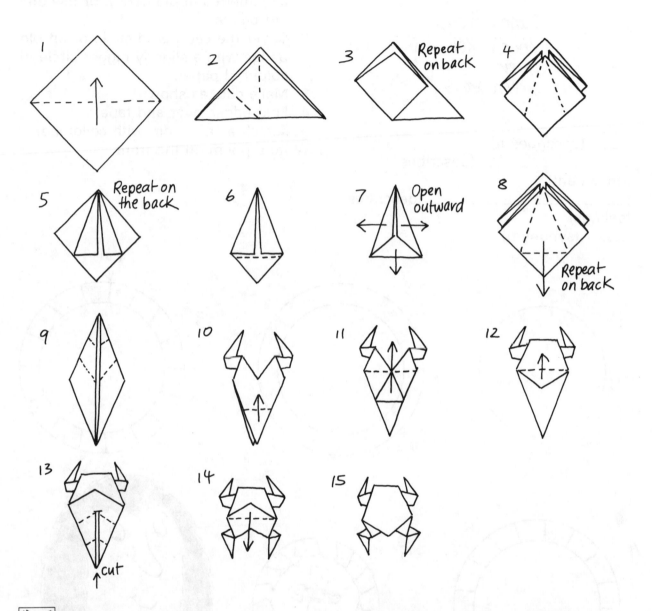

Bibliography

Australian Crocodiles, Turtles and Tortoises, Bay Books, 1981.

Drew, David, *Tadpole Diary*, Methuen, 1987.

Hogan, Paula Z., *The Frog*, Raintree, 1979.

Moffatt, Frank, *Farmer Beans and the Pantry Frog*, Nelson, 1985.

Pinchin, Rebecca, *Frogs*, Hodder and Stoughton, 1986.

Roennfeldt, Robert, *Tiddalick, the Frog who Caused a Flood*, Penguin, 1980.

Schubert, Ingrid, *The Magic Bubble Trip*, Hutchinson, 1987.

Storr, Catherine, *It Shouldn't Happen to a Frog*, Macmillan, 1984.

Growing Things

Introducing Growing Things

Begin this theme with some experiments.

Growing Things in Dark and Light
You need a shallow baking dish lined with cottonwool. Sprinkle different kinds of seeds onto the cottonwool, and dampen with water.

Cover some of the seeds with a dark cone. Keep cottonwool damp.

Watch as the seeds grow, but do not remove the cone for several days. Children predict growth patterns and how those seeds under the cone will look.

Record their predictions and illustrate the outcome of the seed growth.

A Terrarium
Make a terrarium using a plastic lemonade bottle. Remove the black plastic bottom and fill with potting mix. Plant seeds and small cuttings, and then water.

Cut the top off the upper part of the bottle. The domed lemonade bottle fits over the plants and into the black plastic planter to complete the terrarium.

Discuss and compare the growth. Why doesn't the terrarium need watering? Observe condensation.

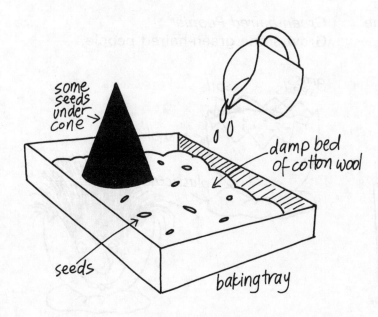

some seeds under cone

seeds

damp bed of cotton wool

baking tray

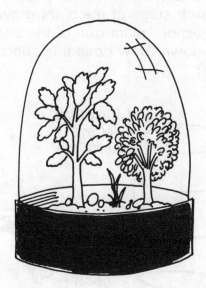

A Green Spider

Tie a length of string to a sea sponge. Attach eight pipe cleaner as 'legs', and two buttons as eyes.

Wet the sponge and sprinkle cress seeds all over so that they rest in the holes and hollows of the sponge. Hang the sponge and keep it damp with a water spray. Wait for the cress to sprout. The spider grows hairy!

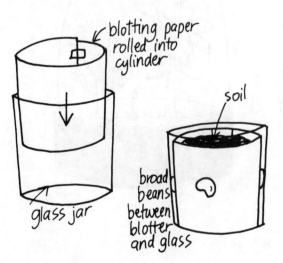

Watching Broad Beans Grow

You will need blotting paper, straight sided glass jars, potting mix, broad beans, and brown or black paper. Chart each stage of the plant growth.

Suggestion: plant one of the seeds upside-down. How does this affect the growth?

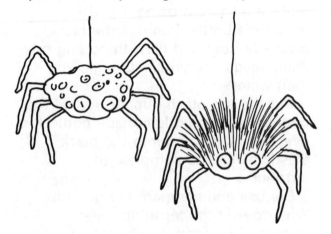

Growing Seeds in Different Media

You will need four saucers. Put cotton wool in one, soil in the second, sand in the third and sawdust in the fourth. Sprinkle with seeds and dampen. Children predict which will grow best. Record growth in a series of pictures or take photos and make an experience book.

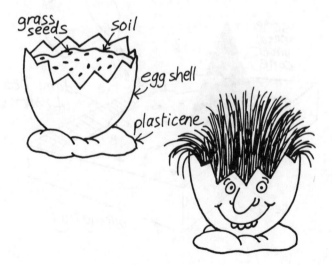

Suggestion: prepare 2 of each of the above saucers, and vary the type of water given to the plants, for example, salty, sugary, muddy.

Green-haired People

Grow some green-haired people.

Root Vegetables in a Jar
Try growing onions and sweet potatoes in a jar of water. Fill jars with water and sit vegetables upright in jar opening. Chart growth.

'Growing' Yeast
Bake bread rolls and watch the yeast 'grow'.

To make 2 dozen rolls you will need:
  1 sachet dried yeast
  1/4 cup warm water
  1 cup of warm milk
  1 teaspoon of salt
  1 1/2 tablespoons of sugar
  1/2 cup oil
  3 eggs slightly beaten
  4-4 1/2 cups plain flour
  1 beaten egg and sesame seeds

1. Sprinkle yeast onto the warm water. Stir until dissolved. Add milk, salt, sugar, oil and eggs.

2. Mix in half the sifted flour and beat until smooth and elastic. Add more flour, one cup at a time, mixing in enough to make a smooth dough which leaves the side of the bowl.

3. Knead dough on a lightly floured surface until smooth and shiny. Put the dough into a large lightly greased bowl, turning the dough so that the greased part is on top.

4. Stand the bowl in a warm place (in an electric frying pan). Cover and leave until the dough has doubled in bulk, (i.e. 1/2 - 3/4 hour).

5. Punch dough down with fist, lightly knead in the bowl for a minute. Divide into 24 equal portions and form each into a bun. Arrange on a greased baking tray and flatten slightly. Cover with a cloth and leave to rise again for approximately 20 minutes.

6. Brush with beaten egg, sprinkle with sesame seeds and bake in a moderate oven for 10—15 minutes.

Classroom grown alfalfa seeds could be used as part of the filling when it's time to eat the rolls

Growing Sprouts

Soak about 3 tablespoons of alfalfa seeds in a jar of cold water overnight. Drain water away completely. Cover the mouth of the jar with a piece of open weave fabric secured with an elastic band. Leave the jar on its side on a window sill but not in direct sunlight.

Rinse the sprouts and drain thoroughly first and last thing each day. (This removes the enzymes and will prevent the sprouts fermenting.)

When tiny leaves form it's harvest time! Other seeds to sprout are mung beans, wheat, and lentils.

Growing Moula

Moisten a stale slice of bread.
Leave for half an hour in the open before putting it inside a plastic lunch box or a plastic bag.

Put the box or bag in a warm dark place. Check daily and observe the growing mould with a magnifying glass. Record the growth and changes over about 5 days.

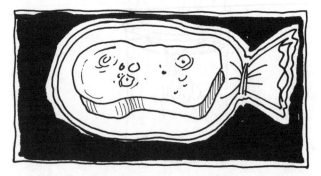

Vary the procedure by using half an orange instead of the bread.

Grow a Crystal Garden

Cover the bottom of a foil pie tin with pieces of charcoal. Mix together 1/2 cup of water, 1/2 cup of salt, 1/2 cup liquid blue detergent and 1 cup of ammonia. Pour this mixture over the charcoal, making sure that it all gets wet. Squirt a few drops of green, blue and yellow food colour onto the charcoal. Leave the dish overnight in a place where it will not be disturbed.

Crystals should have begun to grow by the next day.

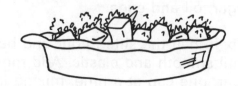

Class Discussion: The Growing Person

Teeth
Talk about teeth.
- What are baby teeth?
- Why do they fall out?

Plaque grows on teeth.
- What is it?
- What will it do if it is left there?

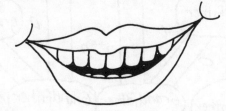

Height
Make a chart to record the heights of children. Measure height at monthly intervals.
Weigh them too!
Read *Tom Thumb* and *Inch Boy*, (see *Bibliography*).

Hair
Talk about hair growth and having a haircut. Write about having a haircut.
Read *Rapunzel* and the poem 'Hair' by Max Fatchen.
Toenails and fingernails grow too!

 ## Research: Growing Food

Discuss people who grow things. For example, the farmer and the orchardist grow plants and animals. Compile lists of all the foods grown on the farm or in the orchard.
How does this food get to us?
What changes does food go through from farm to table?

Assign each pair of children a food product such as corn flakes, tomato sauce, or baked beans. They are to find out about the product.
- Where did the raw material begin?
- How was it grown?

The processing:
- What is used in the processing?
- Are there undersirable additives?
- What effect will these additives have on our growth?

Animal Families
Compile lists of animal families.
Read about and discuss the birth and growth a baby animal, for example, the birth of a kitten.

Life Cycles
Find out about the life cycles of
animals.
Set up a tank and watch tadpoles grow.
(See p. 66)

Set up a mouse house and they'll do it
faster.

Emperor gum caterpillars can be kept
in a tank, too.

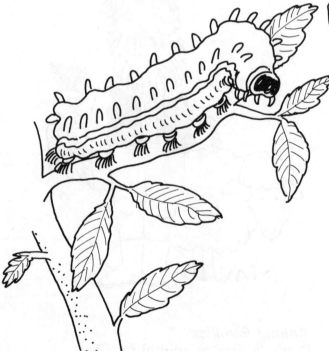

Talk about the human life cycle.

Things That Grow

The family grows. Plot the growth of
the children's families on family trees.

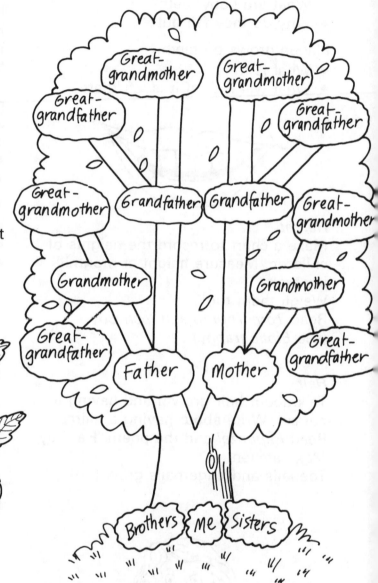

Buildings grow. Observe the
construction of a building in the local
area. Photograph the stages of the
construction.
In the classroom build towers with
blocks, plastic constuction materials,
milk cartons or old Cuisenaire rods.

Art Topics

When I grow up.

Tall and short people.

fan-folded paper so the person "grows"!

Our Painted Garden
Each child paints a part of a garden on a paper panel which is assembled into a mural.

Word Study: Words Grow

Word building activities: take a word and change its meaning by building on letters. For example, dig, digs, digger, digging, 'diggingest'.

Read *The digging-est dog*, by Al Perkins (see *Bibliography*).

Write about:
- the scratchingest cat
- the swimmingest fish
- the gallopingest horse.

Growing Words
Plant some words and watch them grow. Seedlings planted in the shape of words such as a child's name, will become a floral signature.

A Story Grows
Try oral storytelling/making. One child or the teacher provides the first sentence for a story. In turn, each person in the group adds a sentence to continue the story.

Use a tape recorder so that the story can be written down later or kept for future listening.

Writing Starters

- When I grow up.
- The day I shrank to the size of an ant.
- The longest nose in the world.
- From egg to adult: the story of growth.
- The kitten that didn't stop growing.
- My seven metre earthworm.

Collections Grow

Start a collection of pictures of things that grow. Children bring their collections to school:

- stickers
- stamps
- dolls
- toy cars.

I collect soaps and junk mail catalogues!

Bibliography

Carle, Eric, *The Very Hungry Caterpillar*, Penguin, 1980.

Chinery, Michael, *Plants*, Macmillan, 1978.

Cork, Barbara, *Mysteries and Marvels of Plant Life*, Usborne, 1983.

Greenwood, Ted, *VIP: very important plant*, Penguin, 1975

Jack and the Beanstalk, Trad.

Jennings, Terry, *Seeds*, OUP, 1988.

Lionni, Leo, *Swimmy*, Sphere Books, 1977.

McKinlay, Brian, *Growing things: nature studies ideas*, Primary Education, 1979.

Overbeck, Cynthia, *How Seeds Travel*, Lerner, 1982.

Perkins, Al, *The Digging-est Dog*, Collins, 1969.

Rapunzel, Traditional.

Snowball, Di, and Bolton, Faye, *Growing Radishes and Carrots*, Bookshelf, 1986.

Thomas, Ron and Stutchbury, Jan, *Growing Things,* Macmillan Beginners Science, Macmillan, 1989.

Thomas, Ron and Stutchbury, Jan, *Soil,* Macmillan Beginners Science, Macmillan, 1989.

Tolstoy, Alexei, and Oxenbury, Helen, *The Great Big Enormous Turnip*, Pan Books, 1972.

Tom Thumb, Traditional.

Houses

Introducing Houses

Introduce this theme by talking about the houses we live in.
- What are they made of?
- Why do we need them?
- How were they built?

Paint a picture of the house you live in, or take a photograph. Draw a plan of your house.

Make a model of your room using a cardboard box. Show how many windows there are, where the furniture is placed, where the door is, and any other features of your room.

Make the furniture out of match boxes or corks. Measure how long and how wide your room is.

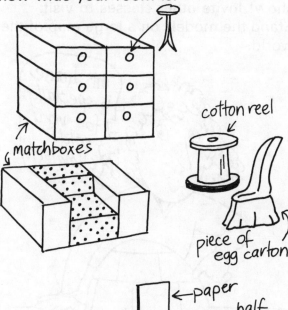

matchboxes

cotton reel

piece of egg carton

paper

half a cork

Talk about the special things in your room. Do you share your room with someone else? What are the good things and bad things about sharing a room?

 ## Find Out About The Neighbourhood

Look at the houses in your neighbourhood.

Make a Map
Make a map of the local area and place the photographs or small sketches of the houses in correct location on the map.

Housing Styles
Classify the different styles of housing in the area.

That's my favourite house!

Make and display sketches of housing styles, for example, Victorian terrace, California bungalow, block of flats, brick veneer, Edwardian and any other styles you can find.

Make a Pictograph

Graph the building materials, or styles and ages of houses in your neighbourhood. Other things to find out about and graph could include:
- the number of rooms in each house which are children's rooms
- the colour of the houses
- the number of storeys of each house and anything else you can think of.

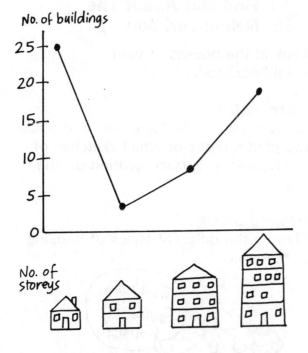

Take a Survey

Survey people in your neighbourhood about their housing preference.
- Why did they choose the area?
- Why did they choose the type of house?
- What would they like to change?
- What is their preferred building material (weatherboard, brick etc)? Why?

- What is their idea of the perfect home?

Research

Houses Around the World

Collect pictures of houses from other neighbourhoods and countries. Children classify the pictures according to their own criteria, for example:
- houses of hot lands
- temporary houses
- houses of cold lands.

Paste the groupings onto large sheets of paper, or paste the pictures onto the paper as a mural.

Make models of houses from around the world. Have an international houses show! Invite other classes to visit. Stand the models on a large map of the world.

Building Influences
Talk about building influences.
What influences the design of houses?
What influences the choice of building materials?

Houses of the Past
Find out about houses of the past.
• How were they built?
• What materials were used, and why?
• Who lived in them?
• How were they kept warm?
• What were bathrooms like?
• What were kitchens like?
• What type of furniture was used?

Corrugated iron house (1870s)

An Early Australian Settlement Village
Children research the styles of houses built in 19th century Australia:
• colonial Georgian
• wattle and daub
• corrugated iron
• Victorian terrace
Make cut out models.
Include churches, shops, blacksmith forge, schools and hotels.
Arange the cut-out models in the village. Include cardboard cut-outs of people in the dress of the period.

Talk about the good and bad aspects of living in:
• a medieval castle
• a bedouin tent
• a prehistoric cave
• a Roman villa
• a stone cottage with a thatched roof
• a wattle and daub hut
and so on.

Houses on the Move
Talk about, collect pictures, draw, paint and make models of:
• caravans
• trailer homes
• houseboats
• tents
• tepees
• junks
• sampans
• covered waggons.

Erect a tent in the room and use it as a quiet reading area.

Temporary Houses

Find out about temporary houses such as:

- Eskimos' igloos
- Aboriginal bark shelters
- European mountain hut for shepherds
- African grass huts.

Why do people build temporary shelters?

What sort of life style do they lead?

The Homeless

Find out and talk about the reasons why some people don't have homes to live in.

- Where can they shelter?
- Whose responsibility is it to provide shelter for the homeless?

Squatters

Debate the issue of modern-day squatters.

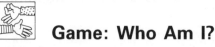

Game: Who Am I?

A child describes the house he or she lives in, its location and other relevant clues. For example: my house is a temporary one. It's made from the skins of animals. The skins are placed over a wooden framework. It keeps out the cold wind, even in summer. The skins are reindeer. I live in Lapland.

'Who am I?' games can also be played about the people who build houses, for example carpenters, architects, plumbers, etc.

Research

Famous Houses

Find out about and visit famous houses, such as:

- Como (Melbourne)
- Ripponlea (Melbourne)
- Yarralumla (Canberra)
- Captain Cook's cottage (Melbourne)
- Admiralty House (Sydney)
- Kirribilli House (Sydney)
- Ayre House (Adelaide)
- The White House (USA)
- Buckingham Palace (London)
- 10 Downing Street (London)

Collect pictures of these and other famous houses. Find out about their history.

- Who designed them?
- What architectural style was used?
- What are the special features?
- What building materials were used?
- Who are the residents?

Houses in Stories

Find out about houses in stories:
- The house that Jack built
- Green Gables
- House at Pooh Corner
- Little House on the Prairie
  Find out about fairytale castles and houses:
- Sleeping Beauty's castle
- Camelot
- Rapunzel's tower
- Three bears' house
- The three little pigs' houses
- Cinderella's house
- The gingerbread house

Model Story Houses

Make models of these and other fantasy houses. Make a fairytale village that includes all of these houses from stories.

Shoe House

Read the traditional rhyme, *There was an old woman who lived in a shoe.* Cut a large outline of a shoe house from thick cardboard. Cut out the windows and door. Turn a corner of the room into the shoe house.

Cooking

A Gingerbread House

Make a gingerbread house.

Ingredients

175 g self-raising flour
100 g plain flour
1 1/2 tblsp. powder ginger
1 1/2 tspn. cinnamon
1/4 tspn. ground cloves
100 g caster sugar
75 g butter
1 egg
1/2 cup golden syrup
1/4 cup treacle

1. Sift together both flours and spices, and stir in caster sugar. Rub the butter into dry ingredients (i.e., flour, spice, caster sugar mix). Mix egg, golden syrup and treacle together and pour into the flour mixture. Mix to a smooth dough, wrap in plastic and chill for 30 minutes.

2. Roll the dough to 1 centimetre thickness. Use the guide below to make the house pattern. Place paper patterns onto the dough and cut.

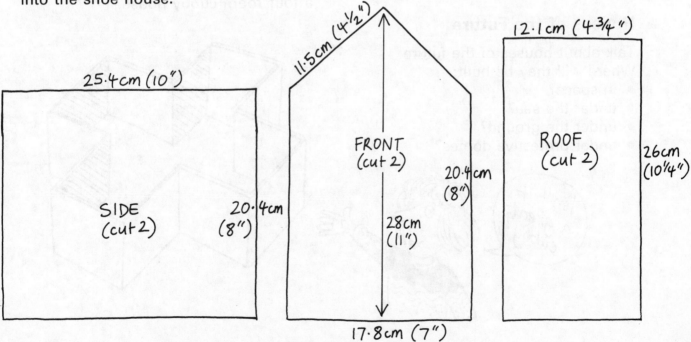

3. Place dough shapes onto a greased baking tray and bake in a moderate oven (180°C) until the edges begin to darken slightly (approximately 25–30 minutes).
4. When cool, apply icing decorations or stick on lollies using the icing as 'glue'.
5. When the decorations are set, assemble the house by joining the walls with icing. When the joins are set, attach the roof sections with icing 'glue'.

Houses of the Future

Talk about houses of the future.
Where will they be built:
- in space?
- under the sea?
- under the ground?
- under protective domes?

A Futuristic House
Design a house of the future.
Draw the plan. List the materials to be used in the construction. Design the furniture and the appliances.

Write an advertisement for this house.

Design a futuristic labour-saving device or a robot:
- What can it do?
- How does it work?

Building Houses

Build a Cubby
Use four large cardboard boxes to build a four room cubby house.

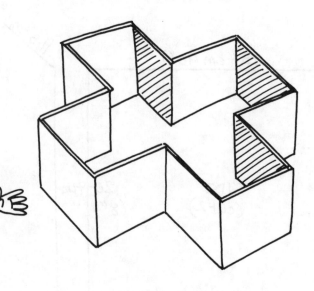

Build a Junk House

This can be built with an old door, or a wire bed base, or a wooden packing case. Old cupboards, tables and other pieces of furniture are attached.

A beach umbrella can be used to make a domed roof and sheets of plastic can be used to complete the covering.

A Mud Brick House

The class can make mini-mud bricks using matchboxes as moulds. Make mud and add grass or straw to bind the mixture. Fill each matchbox with the mud mixture and level.

Turn the mud bricks out of the moulds and set to dry in the sun.

Construct a house using more mud as mortar.

Window and door frames can be made of balsa, the roof can be thatched using grass or straw, or tiled with hand-made clay tiles.

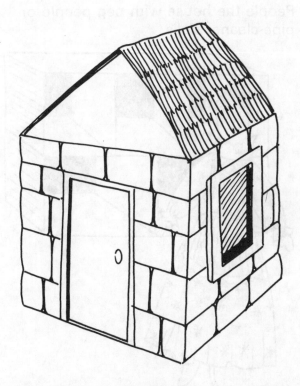

Assemble a village of these mud brick houses and plant a garden around them.

Make a Doll's House
Use cardboard boxes: single storey or double storey? Each group might make a different room and then assemble all of the rooms into one large house. Design and make the furniture. (See p. 77)
People the house with peg people or pipe-cleaner dolls.

A doll's house on a revolving platform.

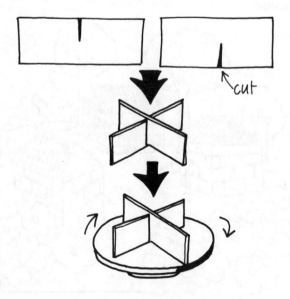

Sand Castles
In the sandpit, build castles, construct roads, villages and other environmental features.
Invent games and make up stories about the castle and the village.

Games

Poor House
Players in pairs sit on chairs in a semi-circle. One pair is seated at the open side of the semi-circle. This is the 'poor house'.
Each couple is numbered, including the poor house couple. One of the poor house pair ask the other, 'If you were not living in the poor house, where would you rather live?'
Partner replies with two numbers, for example, 1 and 5, whereupon couples 1 and 5 change places. The poor house couple tries to get to the chairs vacated by either couple. The couple left without seats become or remain the poor house couple.

Teacher can occasionally call out 'house on fire' and all couples must change seats.

Collect pictures of houses for sale and have children write their own 'honest' advertisements.

House Hunting
Players sit in a circle on chairs with one chair vacant. House hunter is in the centre of the circle looking for a home. Whenever the house hunter moves to a chair the player on the right of the vacant chair moves into it and the rest of the circle moves up one. When player in the centre eventually finds a chair, the player who vacated it becomes the house hunter.

Real Estate
Collect the real estate advertising section from a newspaper. Analyse the language used.

Visiting Speaker

Invite an auctioneer to visit your class to talk about the job of an auctioneer.

Discuss the language, routine, and process of auctioning.

Hold auctions for common place things such as books, pencils and other classroom objects.

School for Sale
Plan an auction campaign to sell the school, including the teachers and students, and all equipment and facilities.

Milk Carton Skyscrapers

Make a city of tall buildings. Cover the milk cartons with papier-mache so that they can be joined and painted. How tall a building can be constructed using milk cartons?

Incorporate appropriate foundations to ensure and maintain the stability of the skyscrapers.

Use the skyscrapers to construct a model city that the children will have to live in. What facilities will they require in a high-rise city?

Plan the transport system. Where will they place shops, playgrounds, parks, hospitals, museums and so on?

Game: House of Cards

Individually or in groups, children build houses of cards. Which child or group can use the most cards to build the highest house?

Research: Animal Homes

Make a list of wild animals and the names of their homes in the wild. Talk about:

- how animal homes are constructed
- which species construct homes
- is the male or the female the home builder?
- what is the purpose of it?
- how does the animal protect the home: by location? camouflage? protective devices?

Talk about the houses that people provide for domestic animals.

Investigate housing of animals in zoos and sanctuaries.

Animal Houses in the Classroom
Build a luxury mouse-house, or a handsome hutch for some guineapigs, or a super aviary for canaries.
Build a bird shelter to hang from a tree in the schoolyard.

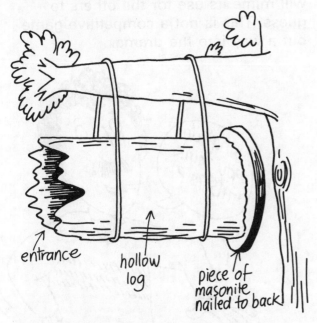

entrance   hollow log   piece of masonite nailed to back

 ### Research: The House Building Process

With luck, a new house will be built near the school. Visit it at regular intervals to observe the progress. Take photos. Use these photographs to illustrate your experience book. Try sequencing, using the photos.

Talk to the workers. Who else works on the house that you don't see? Arrange for guest speakers such as architects and plumbers to visit the classroom to talk about the house building process.

Write descriptions of the workers. Describe the tasks each worker performs. Describe what they wear, the tools they use and their method of work. Draw a series of pictures to show the sequence of work.

Find out about the regulations which affect the building industry in your local area.

Look at old photos of the local area.
- How has the area changed?
- How have houses changed?

Oral History
Talk to elderly people in the area and find out about the changes that have taken place over the last 50 years or so.

Build a Model Town

Children, in pairs, are supplied with client profile cards. Each card gives details about the people for whom a house is needed in the town. For example:
- an elderly couple who want to establish a large garden
- a man and his two teenage children
- a family with four children, two parents and a grandparent and so on.

The children, acting as architects, will determine the needs of their clients and design the house to suit their needs.

They will also design the recreational facilities, shops and other services required by their clients.

On a large blank map, they will locate the houses that they have designed, and build a town.

Seat the children in a circle around the imaginary trunk. You open the trunk and take out an object and mime what the object is used for. The children have to guess what the object is. In turn each child will find an object in the trunk and will mime its use for the others to guess. This is not a competitive game but a way into the drama.

Drama: Visit an Old House

Gather together stimulus pictures of old houses. Discuss them. Together with the children, select one of the houses and visualise a 'journey' through it.

The children silently enact this journey as the teacher describes the progress. For example, 'We are walking toward the door, reach forward to grasp the big door knob. Turn the knob . . . it's very stiff . . . now it's turning . . . push the door open . . . listen to the creaking hinges . . . it's a heavy door . . . push . . .', and so on, continuing the journey through this old, dilapidated empty house.

End the journey in the attic or tower where you will discover an old trunk.

If Walls Could Talk
Talk about the saying, 'If only these walls could talk . . .'

In small groups of three or four, children present a brief glimpse of moments the walls of an old house could have seen.

Read chapter 2 from *The Lion, the Witch and the Wardrobe*, by C. S. Lewis, the section where Lucy walks through the wardrobe and finds herself in another world, Narnia.

Discuss 'doorways' into other worlds and times (time warps and time travel from 'Dr Who', for example). In two or three groups of about six or seven, give children some time to discuss and prepare a small scene involving going through a 'doorway' in a large old house and ending up in another world or time. Each scene is presented to the whole class in turn.

Finish this session with a reflection time, when discussion can take place about some of the ideas and concepts raised during the session, and responses can be shared.

Maths: Measuring Areas

Measure the perimeter of:
- a doll's house
- a cubby
- somebody's house.

Measure the area of rooms in:
- a doll's house
- a cubby
- somebody's house.

Gold Rush Shanty Town

Make a Gold Rush shanty town. Pitch tents and construct lean-tos. Dress in colonial costume.

Recreate life in the diggings. Make damper and Irish stew (see p. 144). Do this on a river bank and pan for gold.

Songs

'Little Boxes' by Pete Seeger.
'Here's A House', from *The ABC Useful Book*.

Bibliography

Bosworth, Michael, *Shelter*, Methuen, 1983.

Computer Software, *Prologic, Designing an energy efficient house.*

Furniss, Elaine and Abrahams, Hector, *31 Ferndale Street,* Southern Cross, Macmillan, 1989.

Harper, Anita, *How We Live*, Penguin, 1977.

Homes, Junior Topic Sevies, Ashton Scholastic.

Howes, Jim, *A Place For Them All: Animal Homes,* Southern Cross, Macmillan, 1987.

Hudson, Nicholas, *That's our House*, Ministry for Housing, Melbourne, 1986.

Hughes, Shirely, *Moving Molly*, Armada Books, 1981.

Jaques, Faith, *Tilly's House*, Heinemann, 1979.

Karavasil, Josephine, *House and Homes around the World,* International Picture Library, Macmillan, 1983.

Langley, Andrew, *Working on a building site*, Wayland, 1983.

Lewis, C. S., *The Lion, the Witch and the Wardrobe*, Lion Books, 1950.

Lionni, Leo, *The Biggest House in the World*, Andersen Press, 1978.

Lobel, Arnold, *Ming Lo moves the Mountain*, Macrae, 1982.

Looking back at Houses and Homes, Macmillan, London, 1988.

McGregor, Peter, *A Roof over our Heads,* Southern Cross, Macmillan, 1987.

McGregor, Peter, *Five Thousand Years of Building,* Southern Cross, Macmillan, 1987.

Milne, A. A., *The House at Pooh Corner*, Methuen Chidren's Books, 1974.

Montgomery, L. M., *Anne of Green Gables*, Angus and Robertson, 1981.

Moorcraft, Colin, *Homes and Cities*, Watts, 1982.

Morrissey, D. W., *Homes*, Macmillan, 1984.

Pienkowski, Jan, *Homes*, Heinemann, 1979.

Pigdon, Keith and Woolley, Marilyn, *Is there Room for me?,* Southern Cross, Macmillan, 1987. (Big book and reader)

Politzer, Annie, *Huts and Tree Houses*, Collins, 1974.

Raitt, J. G., *Building a House*, MacDonald, 1983.

Rowland-Entwhistle, T., *Houses and Homes*, Wayland, 1985.

Stafford, Marianne, *Amy's Place*, Nelson, 1980.

Tate, Joan, *The House That Jack Built*, Pelham Books, 1976.

The Book of the House, Benn, 1979.

The House that Jack Built, Ashton Scholastic, 1985.

Thomas, Ron and Stutchbury, Jan, *Building a House,* Macmillan Beginners, Macmillan, 1988.

Weston, Graham, *In the Home*, Wayland, 1982.

Wilder, Laura Ingalls, *Little House on the Prairie*, Heinemann Education, 1980.

Immenseness

Introducing Immenseness

Read stories, lots of them, about big and small people, (see *bibliography*). Talk about being very small or very big. Write stories about:

- being lost in mum's handbag
- being caught in a spider's web
- being too big to get inside your home.

To get the feeling of being either very big or very small construct some everyday objects on a huge scale, such as a 2 metre tall vase made of boxes and filled with enormous paper flowers, or have the children moving around doll's house furniture set up in the classroom. (See p. 84)

Talk about the relationship between the size of other objects and the people who use them. For example, how big would the owner of the vase be? How big are the people who use the doll's house furniture?

Make up a wall story about the day the owner of the vase came to visit, or about living in a doll's house with the owners.

Imagine Being Very Small

How do we look after the tiny people who live in the doll's house in the classroom? Go on to write a series of adventures for them.

- What happens after we all go home from school?
- What do they do on the weekend?
- The day the mouse escaped from its cage and attacked them.

Read *The Ant Explorer* by C. J. Dennis (see *Bibliography*).

Talk about how the ant felt. Map his journey. What other journeys could the ant take? Write about them and make models of them.

Imagine Being Very Big

Build a model village with milk cartons and other boxes.
We are now the giants.
Are we good or bad giants?
How do good giants help the villagers?
How are the villagers threatened by the bad giant?
How do they repay the good giant?
How do they rid themselves of the bad one?

Invent the people who live in the village. Make models of them and write about their family history. Create characters for the people.

Stories About Giants

Make up stories and adventures concerning the village and its inhabitants, and the giants.

Read lots of stories about giants to provide role and story models.

Stories and Thoughts about Giants

What would you do if the giant came to tea? Plan the menu.
What would it eat from, and what would it use as eating utensils?
If it wanted to stay overnight, where would it sleep at your place?
What other difficulties would there be in having a giant at your house?

Word Study: Bigger Than, Smaller Than

Classify big and little, bigger than, and smaller than.

List all the things that are big and small:
- in relation to me
- in relation to a spider
- in relation to an elephant

and so on.

Size reversals
Imagine:
- a giant spider
- a miniature kangaroo
- an enormous mouse
- a tiny hippopotamus
- a short whale
- a long ant.

where's that cat?!!

 Game

What's in the parcel?
Wrap a huge box like a present.
Let the children guess what the present could be if it was given to them, the size they are.

Then they have to pretend that they are giant children. They have to guess what the present could be, now it is very small.

Research: Tall Structures

Build tall towers and other structures with blocks, cartons and other materials.

Set the buildings as problem solving tasks, for example:
- a tall three-sided building
- a building with a window
- a building supported by pillars.

Build a big bridge and test its strength by 'driving' toy cars and trucks across.

Use a variety of building materials to determine the most effective for each task.

Visit Tall Structures
Go and look at tall buildings in your local neighbourhood. Go to the city and visit the tallest building. Go to the top of the building. How does it feel? What do things look like from the top?

Take photographs. Draw pictures from memory on your return to school. Look at aerial photos of your neighbourhood. (The local council will be able to supply aerial maps of the neighbourhood.)

wow!

Model Tall Buildings

Make a collection of replicas of famous buildings and objects, such as the Eiffel Tower, the Sydney Opera House and the 'Leaning Tower of Pisa'.

Or, collect pictures of these famous landmarks.

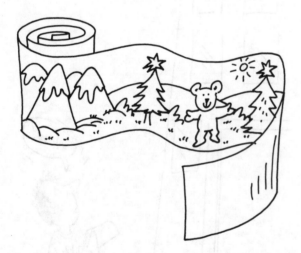

Art

Minimurals

Paint or draw tiny murals on streamer paper or on adding-machine paper rolls.

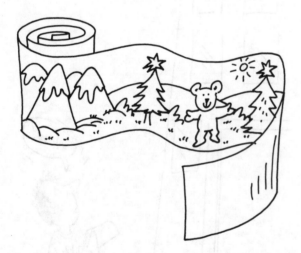

Giant Murals

On huge pieces of paper or on a wall, paint huge butterflies, ants, beetles and other tiny creatures.

Art Starter

Paste a small picture of a person on the paper. Children complete the picture.

Word Study: Size Words

Talk about phrases such as:
- the bigger the better
- good things come in small packages
- pint sized
- giant sized
- big shot
- small-minded
- big-headed
- big top
- little by little
- the little people.

Find synonyms for 'big' and 'little'.

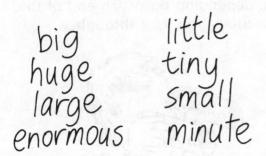

big   little
huge   tiny
large   small
enormous   minute

Make small words from a big word. For example, how many words can you make with the letters in ENORMOUS?

ENORMOUS—
mouse more son
room   soon sure
run   rose sore
sun   sum   snore...

Take a small word and make it big, bigger, biggest by adding on letters.

great greater greatest
light lighter lightest
dark   darker   darkest

Research: Smaller Parts

Look inside everyday objects to see the smaller parts that make it work, for example, inside a clock or a watch, a radio or a mechanical toy.

Talk about the people who work with tiny things, such as the watchmaker, the jeweller, the microchip maker and so on.

Construction Activity
Each child makes a component. Join all the components to form a giant machine. Invent a use for it.

Drama: Many Components Make One

A similar activity can be done in Drama, illustrating the fact that many small components can become a large unit. Children sit in a circle, and one child goes into the centre, forms a 'shape' and begins a simple, repetitive movement, for example, kneeling, body bent over, one fist thumping ground in regular rhythm.

95

One by one, fairly rapidly, children join on by making a body shape that interlocks or relates in some way to someone else's. When they are all in position and moving together, 'freeze' the action. Have each child think of a sound that relates to his or her movement, then 'start' the machine up, with the full sound effects. 'Freeze' the action once again, and this time, children think of a word that relates to the movement, such as 'thump' or 'shhhh'. Start the machine up again.

Now speed it up. Slow it down, then slower, and slower until it breaks down and stops.

Think of a product the machine is making, or a task it is performing.

Class Discussion: Huge and Tiny Things

Look at stamps and discuss the tiny pictures on them. Design a set of stamps for your school.

Look at Big Books and tiny books! Compare them. Make your own.

Make big things small, and small things big, depending on which end of the binoculars you look through.

Use a Magnifying Glass
Use a magnifying glass to look at grains of sugar and salt, fingerprints, tiny seeds, and so on.

Look at things that are too small to see through a magnifying glass. Examine a hair, a fly's leg, and a bit of a spider's web.

Stilts
Walking on stilts makes you taller!
Provide stilts and practise stiltwalking.
Make jam tin stilts.

Bibliography

Dahl, Roald, *The BFG*, Penguin, 1984.

De Paola, Tomie (reteller), *Fin M'coul; the giant of Knockmany Hill*, Andersen, 1981.

Dennis, C. J., *The Ant Explorer*, Macmillan, 1988.

De Paola, Tomie, *The Mysterious Giant of Barletta*, Andersen, 1984.

Leeson, Robert, *The Reversible Giant*, Collins, 1988.

Leggas, Nanice, *The Giant and the Watchmaker's Wife,* Southern Cross, Macmillan, 1989.

Miyoshi, Sekiya, *David and Goliath*, Methuen, 1984.

Muller, Robin (reteller), *Mollie Whuppie and the Giants*, Ashton Scholastic, 1982.

Teale, Sarah, *Giants*, Allen and Unwin, 1979.

Three Billy Goats Gruff, Traditional.

When Goldilocks Went to the House of the Bears, Traditional.

Journeys

Introducing Journeys

Begin this theme by swapping anecdotes of journeys undertaken. Discuss reasons for journeys. For example:

- holiday
- to visit someone
- parent changing job
- moving house
- to visit a famous place.

When we went to visit my Gran in Mildura we had a big adventure!

How do we prepare for a journey:

- clothing?
- mode of transport?
- luggage?
- money?
- food?
- equipment?
- documentation?
- tickets?
- maps?
- household arrangements during absence, such as care of garden, security, pets, mail and so on?

Plan a Journey

Use a map to plot the route. Decide on the mode(s) of transport that will be used. For example:

Prepare a list of equipment, clothes, and so on that will be needed. Organise the trip. Shop for it. Buy tickets. Hire equipment. Plan an itinerary. Arrange accommodation.

Use travel guides, brochures and books written about the places to be visited. Write a diary of the trip. Illustrate with 'photos' and 'souvenirs'.

Use frozen frames technique (tableaux) to illustrate the 'postcards' sent home during the journey.

Groups decide on the 'picture' and pose themselves accordingly, frozen in position. One member of the group can 'read' what is written on the back of the postcard. For example, climbing Ayers Rock is the frozen picture.

📖 Reading About Journeys

Read about the following journeys:
- the voyage of the Kon Tiki
- the race to the South Pole
- up Mount Everest with Hillary
- Burke and Wills across Australia
- crossing the Blue Mountains
- Cook's journeys
- Christopher Columbus to America
- the Pilgrim fathers
- Marco Polo to China
- Vasco da Gama
- Amelia Earhart

Fictional journeys
Find out about fictional journeys.
For younger children try:
- *Jack and the Beanstalk*
- *The story of Ping* by Flack
- *Tom Thumb*
- *The Tale of Peter Rabbit* by Beatrix Potter
- *Possum Magic* by Mem Fox
- *Mr Gumpy's Outing* by Burningham
- *Felix and Alexander* by Terry Denton.

For middle school try:
- *James and the Giant Peach* by Roald Dahl
- *Inch Boy* by Junko Morimoto
- *27th Annual African Hippopotamus Race* by Morris Lurie
- *The Wizard of Oz* by Baum
- *Mulga Bill's Bicycle* by Banjo Paterson
- *The Ant Explorer* by C.J. Dennis

For upper school try:
- *The Boy Who was Afraid* by Sperry
- *The Incredible Journey* by Burnford
- *The Homecoming* by Voigt
- *My grandma live in Gooligulch* by Graeme Base
- *Jason and the Search for the Golden Fleece*
- *Ulysses' journey home from Troy*
- *I am David* by Holm

Journeys in Stories

After reading stories which have journeys in them...

Make Story Maps
Children chart the journey undertaken by the main character or characters.

A Journey Sequence

Children complete the sequence chart as a writing task or as a series of labelled illustrations.

Letter Writing
Write a letter that the main character might have written at some stage of the journey, for example, a letter Ulysses wrote about his encounter with the Cyclops.

Board Games
Make a board game to sequence the story.

Writing on from the Story
Write:
- other adventures the characters of the story might have had
- alternative endings
- your own story about a journey
- a story where the characters from different stories go on each other's journeys. For example, Dorothy goes to the land of the Wild Things instead of Max. Max goes into Mr McGregor's garden instead of Peter Rabbit.

Dramatise episodes of the journey

Read about Time Travel
- *Playing Beatie Bow* by Ruth Park.
- *The Time Machine* by H.G. Wells.
- *A Wrinkle in Time* by L'Engle
- The *Dr Who* stories.
- *Tom's Midnight Garden* by Spence.
- *Half Magic* by Eager.
- *Flying Backwards* by Giles.

Back in Time
- Design a time machine.
- Write about a journey back in time.
- Draw a picture of yourself trapped in time (either forward or backward) dressed as you are now.

 Research: Migration

Interview people who have taken a journey from another country to Australia.
- Why did they come here?
- How did they come here?
- How is Australia different/similar to their original country?
- What was the journey like?
- How did they travel?
- How long did it take?
- Who came with them?
- Did they stop in any other places on the way?
- Do they have any photos of the journey?

and so on.

 Bibliography

Archer, John, *A History of Australian Transport*, Southern Cross, Macmillan, 1989

Baum, L. Frank, *The Wizard of Oz*, Ballantine Books, 1980.

Burnford, Sheila, *The Incredible Journey*, Hodder and Stoughton,

Cramer, Debbie, *Australian Explorers*, The Australian Colour Library, Macmillan, 1985.

Dahl, Roald, *James and the Giant Peach*, Penguin.

Denton, Terry, *Felix and Alexander*, Oxford University Press, 1985.

Ingpen, Robert, *The Voyage of the Poppy Kettle*, Rigby.

Keys, Jane, *The Explorers*, Southern Cross, Macmillan, 1989.

Ransome, Arthur, *We didn't mean to go to sea*, Penguin.

Swift, Jonathan, *Gulliver's Travels*.

Tolkien, J.R.R., *The Hobbit: or There and Back Again*, Allen and Unwin.

Verne, Jules, *Around the World in Eighty Days*.

Kangaroos, Koalas and Other Australian Animals

Introducing Australian Animals

Begin this theme by discussing and finding out:
- What are mammals?
- What are marsupials?
- What are monotremes?
- What are reptiles?
- What are the features of each type of animal that distinguishes them?

List and classify Australian animals according to these classes.

Find out about the habitats of these animals.

Research: Australian Animals

Questions to guide children's research:
- Where does it live?
- What does it look like?
- What does it eat?
- How does it protect itself?
- What are its enemies?
- When and how does it reproduce?
- Who are the ancestors of the animal? Find out about its evolution.

Plot on a map the distribution of the animal.

Excursion

Visit a zoo or sanctuary and observe the animals. Talk to the people who work with the animals.
- What do they feed them?
- How is the food obtained?
- What are the difficulties and advantages of keeping animals in captivity?
- Do they breed in captivity?

Word Study: Animal Dictionary

Make an Australian animal dictionary. Include words such as:

marsupial   mammal
monotreme   carnivore
herbivore   fauna

and so on.

Compile animal families. For example, buck, doe and joey.

Make up crosswords using only the names of Australian animals.

Make models of the animals, out of clay, dough and plasticene.

Make a classroom fauna park.

Make conservation posters and badges.

Read literature from the Department of Conservation, Forests and Lands.

Aborigines and Australian Animals

Why weren't there endangered species when the Aborigines lived here and hunted Australian animals before white settlement?

Read Aboriginal stories about animals. Look at pictures of cave and bark paintings of animals.

Make an Australian animal alphabet book. Illustrate it in an Aboriginal art style.

Endangered Species

Which Australian animals are endangered? Why are they endangered? Discuss the conservation issues involved, for example, the destruction of habitats, killing for fur, and other issues the children raise.

Which animals are protected? How are they protected? What laws govern their protection, and who sets them? What are the penalties for breaking the laws protecting these species? What are the consequences of breaking the laws, or of not having them at all?

Bibliography

Fox, Mem, *Possum Magic*, Omnibus, 1983.

Hyett, Jack, *Koalas, Wombats, and Possums*, Nelson, 1982.

Hyett, Jack, *The Platypus and other Primitive Animals*, Nelson, 1982.

Kangaroos, Wallabies and Possums, Bay Books, 1981.

McNab, Nan, *A – Z of animals*, Lamont, 1987.

Niland, Kilmeny, *Feathers, Fur and Frills*, Hodder and Stoughton, 1980.

Salmon, Michael, *The Great Tasmanian Tigerhunt*, Lamont, 1986.

Serventy, Carol, *Australian Mother and Baby Animals*, Rigby, 1981.

Stonehouse, Bernard, *Kangaroos*, Wayland, 1978.

Light and Colour

Introducing Light and Colour

Begin the theme on a sunny day. Hose the garden and look for a rainbow in the spray of water. Talk about the colours. Where do they come from?

Blow bubbles and look for the colours. Inside, the colour spectrum can be seen in this experiment.

Place the bowl on a sunny windowsill.

Talk about seeing a rainbow after a shower of rain.

Explain the refraction of light. Demonstrate using a beam of light and a triangular prism.

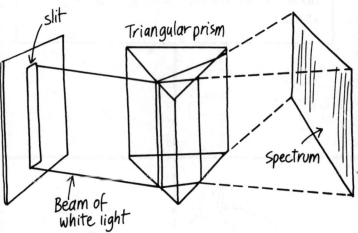

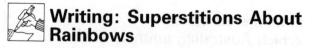

Writing: Superstitions About Rainbows

One superstition about rainbows is 'there's a pot of gold at the end of every rainbow'.

Make up a story about going to find the pot of gold. Make a map showing how you got there.

Read *James and the Giant Peach*, by Roald Dahl, where the peach passes the painters who paint the rainbow.

Experiments

Which colour is white?

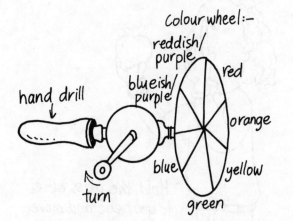

Make a super spinner. Experiment with patterns and a range of colour combinations.

How We see Colour

Talk about how we see colour. After observing and noting the colours in the room, darken the room and observe how the colours fade or disappear.

Now talk about how the eye functions, for example, how it receives the light and relays messages to the brain.

Talk about colour-blindness.

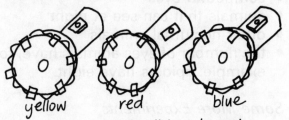

Use sticky tape to stick coloured cellophane over the front of three torches, then shine all three torches on some white paper.

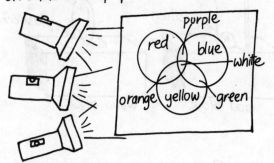

Hold one end in each hand.
Twist the strings to wind it up.
Spread your arms apart
Bring them together..
Apart...
together...

two holes punched in the centre close together

a circle cut out of cardboard and decorated on both sides with crayon, paint or markers.

piece of string about 1.5m long threaded through the circle

A World Without Colour
Look at black and white photos, films and videos. Compare the same video with colour, without colour.

Eye Colour
Survey the colour of eyes among children in class. Graph the results.
   Collect pictures of eye shapes in humans, and in animals and birds. Find out about:
- compound eyes
- animals that can see at night
- other nocturnal animals
- the number of eyes animals have, for example, spiders have eight.

Some More Experiments

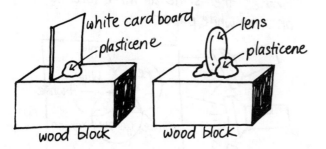

Move the lens towards the card until you see a picture of the candle on the cardboard.

Magnifying With Water
For this experiment, you will need a piece of newspaper, some greaseproof paper and some water. Place a drop of water on the greaseproof paper over the news type. What happens?

Lens Throwing an Image
You will need a magnifying glass and an object for this experiment.

Hold the glass close to your eye and move the object you are looking at towards you.

Optical Illusions

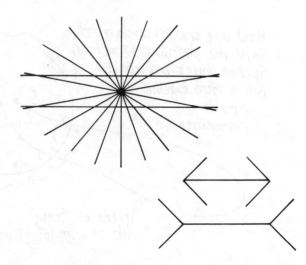

Coloured Spectacles
Make a pair of coloured spectacles, using cardboard, pipe-cleaners and coloured cellophane as glass.

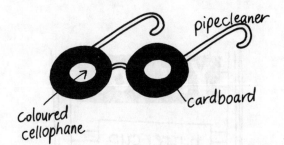

Mirrors and Light: How we see reflections

Game: Kim's Game

Can you remember what you see? Play Kim's game. Place a number of objects on a table. The looker has one minute to see the objects.

Cover the objects and the looker must name or list the objects remembered. (Start with fewer objects. As the children get better at remembering the objects, increase the number of objects.)

Find Out About Lenses

Talk about the use of lenses in everyday objects. Collect pictures of things with lenses.

Look at reflections in other things, for example, a pool of water, a shiny spoon, windows, jars, shiny kitchen utensils, and so on. Discuss convex and concave!

Looking at Kaleidoscopes
Use mirrors and beads to create the principle of a kaleidoscope.

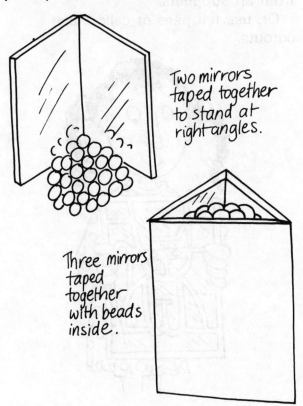

Two mirrors taped together to stand at right angles.

Three mirrors taped together with beads inside.

Research

Find out about the following:
- how colour is used by animals and by people for camouflage
- use of colour on flags
- use of colour on uniforms and sports teams clothes
- colour for safety
- how electric light is made
- photosynthesis
- other kinds of light, for example, glow-worms, luminous, X-ray, neon, and fluorescent
- the history of lighting from prehistoric times to the modern day.

Art

Make stained glass windows.
Paint on the windows or on acetate sheets (shirt box lids). There is paint designed for this purpose available from art suppliers.

Or, use felt pens or cellophane cutouts.

Colour Day

Have a colour day. Declare a yellow day. Wear the colour, eat the colour, list objects associated with the colour. Make a 'yellow ladder'.

Class Discussion

Food and Colour
Talk about the colour of food. How does it make you feel?

Use food colouring to change the colour of the food you eat. Create a blue cake! Black butter! How do the hundreds and thousands look now?

Change the colour of a batch of scones. Are green scones appetising? How about red ones?

Favourite Colours
Discuss favourite colours:
- colour and clothing
- colour and emotion.

Word Study

Discuss and write about the origins of 'colour sayings'.

Or, draw cartoons for them:

- white as a ghost
- green with envy
- blue with cold
- red as a beetroot
- arguing until blue in the face
- black as the ace of spades
- brown as a berry.

Writing

- Write an advertisement to sell a colour.
- The day the world turned red.
- Imagine you live in a land with no colour. Invent a new colour. Where will you use it? Make up a name for it.

Read *The Great Blueness and Other Predicaments* by Lobel.

Bibliography

Andrews, L.W., *Light and Colour*, Raintree, 1978.

Catherall, Ed., *Colours*, Wayland, 1986.

Crews, Donald, *Light*, Greenwillow, 1981.

Getting Started with Themes: Colour, Getting Started, 1980.

Griffiths, John, *Lasers and Holograms*, Macmillan, 1983.

Jennings, Terry, *Light and Colour*, OUP, 1982.

Lewis, Tracey, *Eye Spy*, Collins, 1988.

Lobel, Arnold, *The Great Blueness and other Predicaments*, Collins, 1975.

Pashuk, Lauren, *Fun with Colour*, Hayes, 1985.

Sight, Light and Colour, CUP, 1984.

Testa, Fulvio, *If you take a Paintbrush*, Andersen, 1983.

Thomas, Ron and Stutchbury, Jan, *Light and Colour*, Macmillan Beginners Science, Macmillan, 1989.

Me

Introducing Me

Make a ME book. Write about the public you, that is, 'the me that people see'. Include name, personal deatails such as height, weight, age, colour of eyes and hair, and other personal details. Include also 'My hobbies and sports', and 'The books I enjoy'.

The private ME:
- my likes and dislikes
- my fears
- ambitions
- the things that make me special.

The school ME:
- the way I get to school (draw a map to show the route)
- a map of the school showing my room and the places I play
- my special friends at school
- favourite subjects
- things I like about my school
- thing I don't like
- changes I'd like to make.

ME at home:
- my address
- what my house looks like (draw a plan)
- people who live with me
- my pets
- how I help at home.

- my room
- things my family does together
- my cubby or special place
- my neighbours.

MY I.D:
- fingerprints
- lip print
- baby photograph
- current photograph.

 Art

Make 'Me Cubes'.
Each child decorates a cardboard cube such as a wine cask, with photographs and captions, drawings and magazine pictures which show favourite foods, animals, television shows and personalities.

Include words which tell about 'me', such as funny, bossy, etc. They can also attach objects such as a feather from their pet budgie, a shell they found, and so on.

Completed cubes are hung in the room at a height convenient for the children to examine, compare and discuss.

ME Maths

Graphing Me
Graph the heights of the children. Make a two-dimensional graph.

Each child draws a self-portrait on a given circle of paper or cardboard. Strips of cloth, streamer or paper are attached to represent the child's height. Order from tallest to shortest.

Other things to graphs are:
- eye colour
- hair colour
- nationalities
- birthday months and/or days
- pets
- number of people in family
- favourite colours.

Measuring with Parts of Me

260mm

←size 4→

47mm

185mm

6mm

1302mm

Children use their hand span, stride, foot, and tip of elbow to tip of middle finger (cubit) to measure things such as the classroom, the width of the door, length of a ruler etc.

Discuss variations in measurement when using body parts.

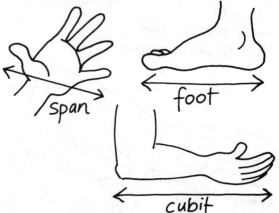

Reason for Standard Measurements
Cut out hand shapes and foot outlines. Arrange in order of size to make a pictograph.

Timing ME
How long does it take to:
- write my name 5 times?
- bounce a ball 10 times?
- run round the oval?
- eat a meal?

John Smith
John Smith
John Smith
John Smith
John Smith

Or, in a minute, how many times can I:
- say my name and address?
- skip with a hoop?
- hop on the one foot?
Extend this activity to Physical Education circuits.

Writing

Keep a Secret Diary for the duration of this theme. Write about:
- friends and enemies
- different feelings experienced
- dreams
- the best and worst thing about each day.

Other diaries or daily recordings could include:
- how much and what TV I watched
- the food I ate
- the books I read
- how many hours I slept
- the games I played.

Research

Children use the following topics to research how their bodies work:
- how I digest my food
- how my blood circulates
- how my body keeps cool
- how my hair grows

- how I breathe
- what my skeleton is like
- how my brain works
- how my body moves
- how many teeth I have and how they grow
- how I see
- how I hear
- how I speak
- how I smell things
- how I taste things.

Art

Hand and Foot Print Casts
Children make foot or hand prints in sand, either individually in an ice-cream container or in the sandpit. Fill the impressions with plaster of paris to make a cast. Let the plaster set.

Or, use wax instead of plaster. Insert a wick before the wax sets to make a foot candle!

Painted Knees Day
Read *Knees*, by Doug MacLeod (see *Bibliography*). Use water-based paints and have a painted knees competition.

Sight

Create a 'fish in a bowl' optical illusion. Draw a fish on one side of a piece of cardboard. On the other side draw a bowl big enough to contain the fish. Stick the cardboard onto a pencil or a piece of thin dowelling. Hold the pencil between the hands and spin the card.

More Optical Illusions

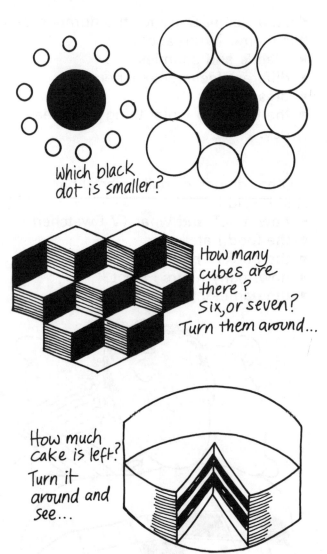

Which black dot is smaller?

How many cubes are there? Six, or seven? Turn them around...

How much cake is left? Turn it around and see...

Blind Tag
Players take up standing positions anywhere in the room. One person is blindfolded and moves around the room attempting to tag the others. Anyone in danger of being caught is allowed to move one, two or three steps, but once a person's three steps are used up, the player must remain stationary. The trick is to take a step only when absolutely necessary. Swaying and crouching are permitted provided that players do not move their feet.

Blindfold Storytelling

Children form pairs. One is 'blind' to be led around by the other, who, whilst giving necessary instructions about steps and turning, also makes up and tells a story about where they are walking, for example, through a forest, or a palace. As trust and concentration grow, they should be able to progress to a stage where physical touching is no longer required.

A Rose-coloured World!

Make cardboard spectacle frames. Make the lenses using red cellophane. Observe the world through rose-coloured glasses. Pipe-cleaners can also be used to make the frames. Try blue cellophane!

Hearing

Play a game of 'Where's the bell?' Sit a blindfolded member of the group in a chair. Other members in turn ring a bell from different places in the room. Can the blindfolded person point in the direction from which the sound comes?

Secret Sounds

One of the group is blindfolded. Other members drop various objects onto a table. The blindfolded one guesses the 'secret sound'.

Sheep and Shepherd

The class, except for two, hold hands to form a circle. The two exceptions stand inside the circle. One, the shepherd, is blindfolded. The other is the sheep and wears a bell around his or her neck. The shepherd must catch the sheep by listening for the sound of the bell.

Zoo in the Dark

The whole group, or part of it, is blindfolded and in pairs. Each pair decides which animal they represent and what sound they make. They are then mixed up by the teacher or unblindfolded people. By making the sound the partners try to find each other.

Mapping Sounds

Take the class for a listening walk around the schoolgrounds or the local environment. On returning, draw a map of the route taken and mark in the locations and sounds heard.

For younger children, a prepared map could be taken on the journey and marked en route.

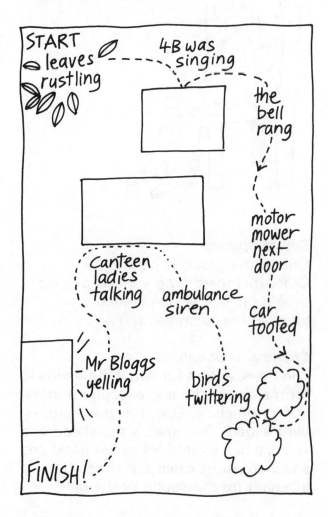

Following a Partner's Direction

Place a screen across a table between partners. One of the partners makes a pattern with attribute blocks or other coloured shapes. Then, this partner gives verbal instructions to the other partner so that the pattern can be recreated on the other side of the screen.

Radio Play Sound Effects

Write a radio play with lots of sounds in it. Work out ways to make the sound effects on tape.

Or, make a tape of different sounds. Ask friends to guess the sound.

Make a Stethoscope or Telephone

You will need some plastic tubing and the top part of two plastic bottles.

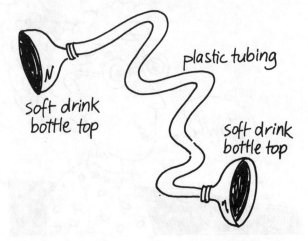

Safe Harbour

One end of the room is designated the 'Harbour', and the other end is the 'Sea', over which there is a heavy fog. Half of the players are spaced over the sea sitting cross-legged as rocks. Once the game starts, the 'rocks' make sounds of waves crashing. The remainder are blindfolded and stand opposite the harbour. They are the 'ships' trying to steer themselves safely into harbour, guided by the sound of the waves on the 'rocks'.

If any 'ship' touches a 'rock' it removes its blindfold and becomes a 'shipwreck'.

Smell

Make aromatic dough flowers.
1. Make a dough by mixing together flour, salt and water.

2. Divide into three portions. To one portion add red food colouring and cinnamon. To another portion, add blue food colouring and vanilla. Colour the third lot green and add eucalyptus oil.
3. Make flowers from the dough. Place the flowers on a greased baking tray and bake until hard. Invent names for the flowers.

Make Rose Water

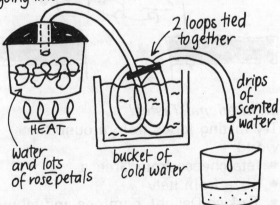

Try the same method using gum leaves or petals from other 'smelly' plants.

Smelly Things
Read *The Smelly Book* by Babette Cole.
Plan an activity about the story.
Make smelly boxes.
Children guess what's in the box.

Taste

Find out and talk about:
- how we taste our food
- which foods taste sweet
- which foods are bitter
- which foods taste sour
- does food taste better when you can smell?

Experiment with Taste
Cut up a lemon and an orange.
Cover your eyes and hold your nose and have a friend put a piece of either in your mouth on your tongue.
Can you tell which one?
What happens to your sense of taste if you suck an ice-cube before tasting the food?

International Tastes!
Try tasting foods from around the world:
- feta cheese from Greece
- pizza from Italy
- Turkish Delight, hommos and tabouli from Lebanon
- spring rolls and fried rice from South-East Asia
- hot dogs and popcorn from USA
- pork pies from England
- souffle, snails and frogs' legs from France
- couscous from Africa.

Describe the tastes.
List words for each taste.

Feeling

Make a collection of hard, rough, smooth, soft, and sharp things.
Make collages using these things.

Sorting by Touch
Make a collection of textures. Have two of each in the collection. Blindfolded, the children must sort the collection into matching pairs.

Feelings and Faces
How does your face show how you are feeling? Invent a simple comic strip story using the facial expressions.

Taking Care of Me

Food Pyramid

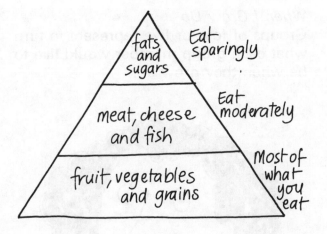

Keep a food diary for a week.
Relate the nutritional values of the food to the food pyramid.

Make a 3D food pyramid.
Paste magazine pictures of foods into appropriate sections of the pyramid.

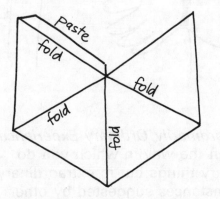

Write an advertisement for radio or television to promote the food pyramid.

Exercise

Set up a fitness circuit around the schoolground.
Record daily times and achievements.
Graph individual improvement.

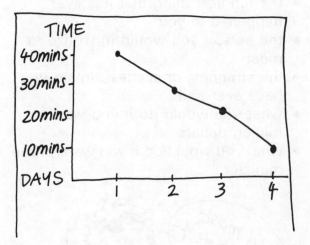

Rest

Survey the members of the family to determine the sleeping times.
Who sleeps most? least?

Writing

Use the following topics to write about 'Me':

- a description of yourself to someone who has never met you
- the funniest thing that has ever happened to you
- the person you would most like to meet
- the strangest or scariest dream you have ever had
- what you would do if you won a million dollars
- what you would do if you were prime minister.

Drama

Re-enacting Dreams
In groups of four or five the children talk about dreams and together invent a dream which they then enact to the other groups.

My Life
A group of four or five devise and present a set of 'photographs' (tableaux) of various events in each member's life.

When I Grow Up
Groups of four or five represent in turn what each group member would like to be when they grow up.

Extraordinarily Ordinary Experiences
Act out the way in which you do ordinary things but in extraordinary circumstances suggested by other members of the group.
For example:
- cleaning your teeth.
  Extraordinary circumstance – you are on a ship in a storm

- writing a message while talking on the telephone. Extraordinary circumstance — you have one arm in plaster
- brushing the dog. Extraordinary circumstance — the dog grows and grows as you brush.

How I Sound and Look

Tape record (audio and/or video) children reading, reciting, talking playing and singing.

Bibliography

About Me, Childcraft, 1980.

About My Body, Ward Lock, 1982.

Alexander, Martha, *When the New Baby Comes, I'm Moving Out*, Dial, 1979

Bennett, Olivia, *Family Life*, Macmillan, 1982.

Branden, Nathaniel, *Honouring the Self*, Bantam, 1985.

Branden, Nathaniel, *How to Raise Your Self-Esteem*, Bantam, 1985.

Cole, Babette, *The Smelly Book*, Cape.

Gyles, Brandreth, *Me! My Book about Myself*, Knight, 1979.

MacLeod, Doug, *Knees*, Penguin.

Riley, Susan, *Angry*, Child's World, 1978.

Roberts, Mary, *What A Birthday*, Southern Cross, Macmillan, 1987.

Stodart, Eleanor, *Alive and Aware*, Hodder and Stoughton, 1978.

Taylor, Ron, *How the Body Works*, Golden, 1981.

Thomas, Ron and Stutchbury, Jan, *Eyes*, Macmillan Beginners Science, Macmillan, 1989.

Thomas, Ron and Stutchbury, Jan, *Ears*, Macmillan Beginners Science, Macmillan, 1989.

Thomas, Ron and Stutchbury, Jan, *The Mouth*, Macmillan Beginners Science, Macmillan, 1989.

Thomas, Ron and Stutchbury, Jan, *The Nose*, Macmillan Beginners Science, Macmillan, 1989.

Thomas, Ron and Stutchbury, Jan, *Skin and Hair*, Macmillan Beginners Science, Macmillan, 1989.

Ward, Brian, *Touch*, *Taste and Smell*, Watts, 1982.

Night and Day

 Drama

Prepare the room so that children enter a darkened room, with appropriate 'dream' music playing: something soft and haunting, or perhaps 'Welcome to my Nightmare' by Alice Cooper.

Children move at random around the space, moving appropriately as you describe a dream sequence: 'you are being chased by something ...but when you try to run you can only go in slow motion. Now the floor is getting softer and is turning into syrup. Look out...the ceiling is getting lower and lower...'(and so on until they are lying on the floor) ...' there's a crack in the wall you can roll through!' Keep this up for about 5 minutes, and end with them sitting quietly on the floor.

In pairs, children tell their partner about a recent or recurring dream. They find a new partner and tell that partner about the dream their first partners told them.

Read *The Dream Eater,* by Christian Garrison, (see *Bibliography*). There are several different versions of this tale.

Play the Dream Eater game: divide the class into 2 groups. One group is arranged along one wall: they are bad dreams trying to get to the other side of the room where imaginary sleepers are. They must pass through the Dream Eaters, arranged in a belt across the middle of the room. The Dream Eaters cannot move their feet, but can wave, bend, and sway as much as they can. They must also keep their eyes closed. The dreams try to get through without being touched: even the slightest touch means the dream is eaten, and they must remain in that position, becoming an added hazard for the others because they are now dream eaters. After all the 'dreams' have been 'eaten', the groups swap roles.

In groups of 4 or 5, children work out a short television commercial advertising dreaming. They will probably need to identify a 'target audience' to help them work somethings out, and this ensures variety. Groups present their advertisements to the rest of the class.

Make bubble print dream creatures: prepare several dishes (with raised edges) containing watery dishwashing liquid and powdered food dye. This mixture is bubbled up by blowing through a straw. When the bubbles are high, a sheet of paper is pressed on the bubbles so that they burst onto the paper. Do not press the paper into the liquid! The bubble prints dry instantly, and another colour bubble print can be made, touching or overlapping the first. After using several colours, children add to and enhance their prints with crayons, turning the shapes into strange creatures.

During this latter process, and while waiting for others to finish, children are talking about their emerging creatures: keep them on the dream track. They can begin making up stories about their creatures.

In groups of about 6, children look at each other's creatures, and share comments and stories about them. Using all the creatures in the group, they build up a 'dream' and work out a small performance piece. They can use the prints solely as a 'starter' or they can use them like puppets or masks, or in some other way.

End the lesson with a reflective time to calm them down, and also to share their thoughts about frightening nightmares and fears at night. Tell a few of your dreams too: the point being that everyone has nightmares.

Discuss

Fear of the Dark

Read *The Owl Who Was Afraid of the Dark*, by Jill Tomlinson (see *Bibliography*), or any of the stories in the Bibliography.

Discuss fear of the dark and why people are afraid. How can these fears be overcome or dealt with? What fears do the children have at night?

Safety at Night

How do we keep safe at night?

- Wearing light colours (be seen, be safe).
- Lights on bikes and fluorescent safety gear.
- Staying where there are lights.
- Safety lights on roadworks and building sites.
- Street lights and external house lights.
- Leaving a light on inside the house; timing switches.
- Lights on tall buildings and steeples (for pilots).
- Lighthouses are safety lights for ships.
- Navigation lights on ships and planes; lights and reflectors on cars.

 ## Art

Night Safety Posters

Make 'Safety At Night' posters. Make up an advertising campaign for various aspects of safety: include advertisements for television and radio.

Night Lights

Make a list of all the sources of night light you can think of. For example: neon signs, candlelight, moonlight, fluorescent lights, car lights, oil lamps, torches, gas lamps and so on.

Collect pictures of lights at night: traffic, neon signs, lights reflected in a river, and so on. Find out about neon light.

- How does it work?
- Why is it called neon light?
- Who discovered/invented it? (Sir William Ramsay)
- What are the advantages of neon light?
- What are the applications of it?

Collect pictures (or take photos) of neon signs. Look at the shapes, words, movement. Find pictures of famous neon lights, for example, at Piccadilly Circus in London, in Tokyo, in Times Square (New York), and the Skipping Girl neon sign in Melbourne.

Draw a picture of a street at night, using a crayon resist technique. The lights are drawn in crayon, and a wash of black paint applied last. (The paints won't take where there is crayon.) Or colour can be thickly applied all over the paper, in colours of the lights desired. A final thick layer of black crayon or pastel is applied, and then the picture is scratched through the black, revealing the colours below.

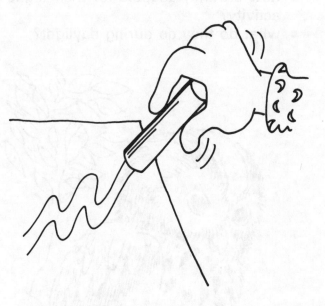

Use these techniques to create pictures of:

- the night sky
- a burglar at work
- homeless people at night
- nocturnal animals.

Research: Nocturnal Animals

Find out about nocturnal animals:
- which ones are nocturnal?
- feeding habits
- habitat
- how are they adapted for their night activity?
- what do they do during daylight?

Visit a zoo or an animal sanctuary that has a nocturnal animal section. Or, participate in nocturnal walks organised by conservation groups.

Nocturnal People!
List the occupations which require people to work at night, for example:
- police and security people
- ambulance workers
- hospital personnel
- bakers
- transport workers
- newspaper printers
- taxi drivers
- entertainers.

Find out about these jobs. List the advantages and disadvantages of working at night rather than during the daytime.

Experiment with Sunlight

Find out about the sun as a source of light and energy.

Take a colour photo of a spot in the schoolground in the morning at 9.00 am. Take another photo of the same spot later in the day, last thing before going home. Compare the differences in the light and colour, shadows and direction of light, and so on.

Explore solar energy.

MAKE A SUN MOTOR :-

The sun warms the cans
The cans warm the air
Then this warm air rises and
makes the motor (pinwheel) turn.

1. Get 3 painted cans, all alike.

2. Cut the tops and bottoms from the cans.

3. Tape the cans together.

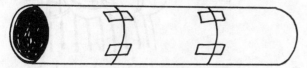

4. Stand the cans on 2 books in front of a window in the sunshine.

5. Get a piece of thin wire (such as twist wire for a plastic bag) and tape a pin to one end. ←pin

6. Tape the wire to the top of the cans

7. Make a pinwheel.

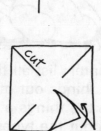

Bibliography

Allen, Pamela, *A Lion in the Night*, Nelson, 1985.

Denton, Terry, *Felix and Alexander*, OUP, 1985.

Ellis, Malcolm (Ed.), *Nocturnals*, Dent, 1979.

Heinz, Kurth, *A Night in Town*, New Puffin Picture Book, 1978.

Lurie, Morris, *Night, Night: Seven Going to Bed Stories*, OUP, 1986.

Mayer, Mercer, *There's a Nightmare in My Cupboard*.

O'Toole, Mary, *One Dark, Dark Night*, Southern Cross, Macmillan, 1987.

Pearson, David, *One Rainy Night*, Southern Cross, Macmillan, 1987.

Pigdon Keith and Woolley, Marilyn, *Early Morning*, Southern Cross, Macmillan, 1987.

Prelutsky, Jack, *Nightmares: Poems to Trouble Your Sleep*, Black, 1978.

Strand, Mark, *The Night Book*, Aurum Press, 1985.

Thomas, Ron and Stutchbury, Jan, *Light and Colour*, Macmillan Beginners Science, Macmillan, 1989.

Tomlinson, Jill, *The Owl who was Afraid of the Dark*, Penguin, 1973.

8. Balance the pinwheel on the pin and watch it turn.

Occupations

Introducing Occupations

Children conduct a survey throughout the school about the jobs of parents.

A Dictionary of Occupations

A

anthropologist

artist

architect

- advertising worker
- airline worker

Architect: look at architectural drawings and plans; look at architectural styles of the area; design a house or building. (See *Houses*, p. 77)

B

butcher

- baker
- bricklayer

Baker: visit a baker or a hot bread shop; watch bread being made; compare bread sizes, shapes and variety; note hygiene and safety precautions; find out about regulations in food preparation areas — who sets them? Why are they important?

C

chef

carpenter

Carpenter: list all the tools used; make some things out of wood; find out about the things a carpenter does; find out about the types of construction.

D

- dentist
- doctor
- delivery man

dog catcher

Dogcatcher: what are the laws in your area regarding dogs? Who makes them? Are they fair? What are the penalties? Visit the Lost Dogs Home. What happens to the dogs when they get there? How do they get there? Ask the RSPCA to provide a guest speaker. Visit a RSPCA shelter and find out about the different jobs people do.

E

egg farmer

- electrician • engineer

Electrician: how does the electricity get into your house? How is a building wired for electricity? How do switches and fuses work? Safety with electricity: design safety posters. Find out about how people lived before electricity. (See *Volts*, p. 181)

F

- farmer
- film maker

factory worker

Factory worker: visit a local factory; observe and discuss the assembly line and the process of raw material to product; what happens to the product after it leaves the factory? Historical aspects: history of factories; child labour in factories.

G

gardener

- grave digger
- garage mechanic

Gardeners: visit council gardens; seasonal jobs of gardeners; what do they do during wet weather? Find out about different types of gardens. Establish and work in the school garden. Why are gardens important? Market gardening. (See *Growing Things* p. 69)

H

Horse trainer: how are horses cared for daily? How are they trained? What do horses do: racing, show jumping, and so on. Is horse racing fair to the horse? Maths: working out the odds. Other people who work with horses. The role of the horse in history: transport, farm work and so on. Breeds of horses, and origins, and their suitability for various activities.

I

History of ice-cream; how it is made; survey to determine favourite flavours; make your own ice-cream; visit the ice-cream parlour and talk to the people who work there; the various shapes and forms ice-cream come in; find out about natural ice-cream and tofu ice-cream. Things you can make with ice-cream: spiders, sundaes, baked alaska, and so on.

J

Journalist: the role of the journalist on a newspaper or magazine; the journalist/reporter collecting news; what happens after the story is handed in; the other people involved in the production of a newspaper. Is there a difference between a print journalist and a television journalist? Produce your own newspaper. Roleplay news events and reporters gathering the story.

K

Key cutter: visit the local key cutting shop and observe; make a key collection of old and new keys; compare shapes and sizes of antique and modern keys; find out about the history of keys; keys for locking and for winding things up; list 'key' words like keystone, keyboard, keynote, keyring, keyhole. 'Getting the key when you're 21': what is the significance? What is the significance of being given the keys to a city?

L

leather worker

Leather worker: sources of leather; tanning process; variety of leather products and their uses; make things out of leather.

M

- minister
- musician

milliner

Minister: other names for people who work in the field of religion — nun, priest, Pope, bishop, ayotollah. Various religions and their festivals, names of their personnel, their places of worship. Famous places of worship. Differences in their beliefs. Prejudice and persecution.

- nuclear physicist
- neurologist

nurse

Nurses: training — types of nursing; famous nurses; history of nursing; nurses in places other than hospitals.

O

- orator
- ornithologist

opera singer

Ornithologist: what does an ornithologist do? List all the occupations that end in '-ist'. Do some ornithology around the local area! Get information from local bird observers' clubs, or the Gould League. Find out about bird species indigenous to your area.

P

•pharmacist
•painter
politician

Pharmacist: visit the local pharmacy; find out about the changed role of the pharmacist; talk about drugs and the rules regarding the taking of them; safety rules regarding drugs in the home; look at the ingredients of common things like shampoo found in the shop; what are prescriptions? What are the laws governing them?

R

road construction worker

•railway worker

Railway worker: visit the railway station; talk to the station master; study maps of the rail network in your area; look at railway timetables, wait for a few trains and test their punctuality; find out about other jobs involved in running a railway service; study the history of railways; build a model railway in your room.

Q

queen

quilt maker

Quilt maker: find out about the history of quilting and quilts; visit a bedding shop and find out about modern equivalents; visit the art gallery to see antique quilts; visit a modern quilters exhibition; invite a patchwork quilt maker to visit and demonstrate the skill; make quilted patchwork squares.

S

•singer
•secretary

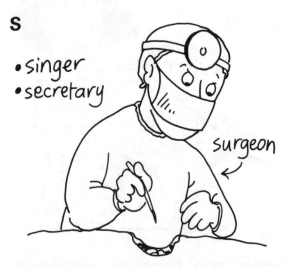

surgeon

Singer: listen to a variety of singing styles and voices; list the different kinds of voices and styles; where do people sing? Find out about troubadours. Find out about different kinds of performances for singers. List famous singers in each category.

T

teacher

• taxidermist • television worker

Television worker: what types of jobs are there in the field? Invite television personalities to be guest speakers. Visit a television studio. How does television work? Survey to find out favourite television shows. Use a video to make a television program: documentary about occupations, quiz show, play, soap opera, etc.

U
• undertaker
• upholsterer

underwear salesperson

Undertaker: what do they do? Ask a local undertaker to visit and talk about the job.

V

• violin maker

vet

Vet: visit the local vet and find out about the job. What is the most common animal treated, and what is the most common complaint? Find out about: veterinary specialists; quarantine stations; farming communities; research centres; zoos.

W

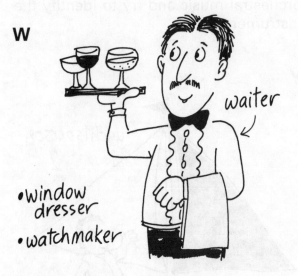

waiter

• window dresser
• watchmaker

Waiter: what are the tasks and skills involved? How do you set a table correctly? How do you serve food correctly? How do they take the orders and remember who ordered what? Find out about suitable attire. How do you treat a waiter? Have a meal in a restaurant. Role play the different people and possibilities involved.

X

xylophone player →

Xylophone player and other musicians in the orchestra: who are the members of an orchestra? Classify the instruments and the specific names of the people who play them. Listen to orchestral music and try to identify the instruments.

Y

yachtsperson

Yachtspersons and other sailors: find out about types of yachts; yachting and sailing terms; history of sailing vessels; jobs of sailors in various types of vessels; models of sailing vessels.

Z

•zoologist

Zookeeper

Zoo keeper/zoologist: go to the zoo and talk to the people who work there.

General Activities

Assign one occupation to each child or pair of children. Get them to find out about: training and preparation for the job; the nature of the job; any hazards or special procedures required; why people choose that job, and their likes and dislikes about the job. Is there a special uniform or special clothing? What equipment is needed? Find out about the roles of males and females in that occupation.

How to Find Out About Jobs
Write letters to Unions or Associations, or places where the people are employed; interview people in that occupation.

Occupations of the Past
Find out about occupations that no longer exist, or exist in a limited fashion, for example, blacksmiths and chimney sweepers. Trace the occupation back to its origins, or early days.

How to Present Your Research
Taped interviews; make displays about the job, including photos taken showing people involved in the job or aspects of the job; recruitment posters; information pamphlets.

135

Pirates

Introducing Pirates

Make a huge skull and crossbones flag. Display it outside the classroom to announce the theme to all who pass. Materials needed: white felt and black hessian.

Pirate-scapes

Transform the room into a pirate environment: ship? cave? inn? Rearrange the furniture, paint the windows as port holes. Furnish with treasure chests, booty, ship's anchor, fishing net, sails, weapons, and other nautical references.

Treasure Maps

Make treasure maps. These maps include landmarks, compass points and distances. Age the map by singeing the edges of the paper with a candle, or by putting it into a hot oven for a short time only (retrieve it before it bursts into flames).

Features of the island to be made and used as props could include cardboard cutouts of trees, a swamp made of a piece of green plastic, rocks made with cardboard cartons covered with crumpled brown paper and so on.

Treasure Island

Mark out an island shape in the playground. Groups of children plan the features of a treasure island on a photocopied representation of the shape. Over the next few days each group, in turn, builds its island on the playground island shape and hides their treasure. They give directions for finding the treasure to the remainder of the class who attempt to locate it. Older children will be able to use compasses to find their way from place to place on the island.

Selling Pirates' Weapons

Design weapons for pirates.
Make models of these weapons, and prepare a catalogue for presentation to a pirate client.

In pairs the children improvise the selling and buying situation. One child is the pirate, the other the salesperson.

Pirate Props
Make treasure chests and the loot. Use cardboard cartons, papier-mache beads, coins, and artifacts. Use to decorate environment and as props for role plays and free play.

Dress-up Day
Create costumes or use those made above in previous activity. The children become their pirate creation.

Provide wigs or make them with wool stitched to a stocking base, false hair and make-up so that they can attach moustaches, eyebrows, scars, and so on. Make eye-patches, wear earrings, scarves and other pirate accessories. Sing sea shanties.

Make red 'rum' cordial and chocolate coins. Make some pirate food.

Pirate Food

Pirate Boat Rolls
Cut some long rolls in half. Put on your favourite filling. Decorate with pirate flags attached with toothpicks.

Treasure Baskets
Cut off the top of a cup cake. Scoop cake out of the centre. Fill with treasure (i.e. Smarties). Put top back on and ice.

Hold a pirate tea party.
Have a treasure hunt for chocolate coins wrapped in gold paper.
Read pirate stories
Tell pirate "tall tales"
Have the cameras ready to capture the day's events for your class newspaper or Pirate Log Book.

Writing

Pirate Codes
Protect your treasure! Use the codes below to write secret messages.

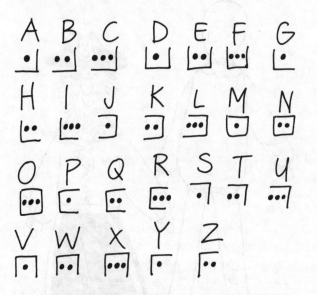

Or use invisible ink: dip a pen in lemon juice before writing the message. The paper has to be heated, for example with an iron, for the words to reappear.

Message in a Bottle
Each child or group writes a message which is from someone marooned or shipwrecked on an island. Place the messages inside plastic bottles and float them in a baby bath. Each group retrieves a bottle and plans a rescue in response to the information in the letter.

Each group presents their plan for consideration by the whole class: a cooperative problem solving session!

Game

Bury the Treasure
Draw a treasure map on a piece of card. Rest the map on 2 supports so that it is a few centimetres above the level of a table. Place a magnet under the map to mark the location of the treasure. Children locate the treasure using a compass.

Walk the Plank
Draw a plank shape on the classroom floor or on the school ground. One by one, blindfolded children walk the plank.

Make a Board Game
In groups, construct a follow-the-trail-type board game which incorporates pirate type catastrophes and good times.

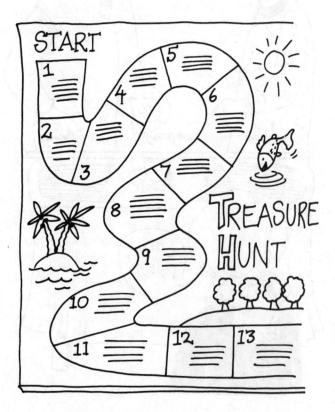

Drama

With the class invent a pirate crew from the captain and first mate down to the cook and the cabin boy.

The children adopt one member of the crew and write a personal profile. Include birth and family details, appearance, personality, likes, dislikes, habits, anecdotes about past life, and so on.

Each child makes a life size doll of the invented crew member. Use pantyhose stuffed with paper. Make the clothes to dress the crew member.

pantihose stuffed with paper

An Alternative Ship's Crew
Cardboard cutout figures can be made to represent each crew member. Paint on the clothes or paste on material.

The figures could be minus heads and then the child inventor becomes the pirate character wearing make up and appropriate headgear.

140

These dolls or cardboard characters can be used to help the children to establish and take on the roles of their pirate creations in role-play situations.
The action could be played out inside the classroom environment or outside on the island.

Marooned Sailor

Pirate crew lands on the treasure island and in the course of exploration they discover an old sailor marooned there. This character can be the teacher in role.

Interviewing for Crew Members

The captain and a select group of crew members interview the remainder of the pirates who present for jobs on board. Interviewers devise questions and tests that they feel are relevant. This activity may also be a writing activity.

Present an advertisement like:

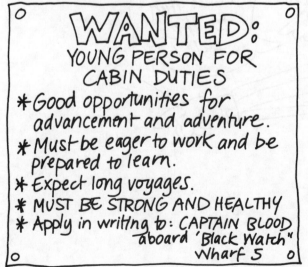

A Retiring Captain

The captain is retiring. Each crew member presents a testimonial at a farewell dinner. A successor has not yet been chosen so each speaker is likely to do a bit of self-promotion during his/her speech.

Secret Signals

Form and develop secret signals and greeting rituals.

Treasure Map

Two pirates argue over the ownership of a treasure map.

Research: Real Pirates

Individually or in groups find out about:
- pirate ships and other sailing vessels of the time
- famous pirates including female pirates
- areas of the high seas where pirates were active
- modern day pirates, for example, hijackers.

Word Study

Compile a dictionary of pirate language:

- heave ho!
- pieces of eight
- aye aye captain
- hoist the mainsail
- Jolly Roger
- Avast there, me hearties!
- Swing him from the yardarm
- Davey Jones' locker
- Shiver me Timbers
- feed him to the fish
- you scurvy dog!
- Ahoy there!
- batten down the hatches
- man overboard
- marooned
- scuttled
- sea-dog
- doubloons
- landlubbers.

Bibliography

Brading, Tilla, *Pirates*, MacDonald.

Fleischman, Sid, *The Ghost in the Noonday Sun*, Penguin.

Hawkins, Colins, *Pirates*, Collins, 1987.

Hutchins, Pat, *One-eyed Jake*, Bodley Head, 1979.

Lloyd, Barbara, *Pirate Edna of Old Tallangatta*, Angus and Robertson.

Loof, Jan, *My Grandpa is a Pirate*, Black.

Mahy, Margaret, *The Pirates' Mixed-up Voyage*, Methuen, 1985.

Martyr, Andrew, *Patch the Pirate Cat*, Hamilton, 1987.

McNaughton, Colin, *Jolly Roger*, Walker, 1988.

Nye, Robert, *Harry Pay, the Pirate*, Knight, 1983.

Older, Jules, *Jane and the Pirates*, Heinemann, 1984.

Ryan, John, *Captain Pugwash Series*, Penguin.

Tennant, Emma, *The Search for Treasure Island*, Penguin, 1981.

Thomas, Ron and Stutchbury, Jan, *The Sea*, Macmillan Black Line Masters, Macmillan, 1988.

Feed him to the fish!

Quiche and Salad: a theme about food

Introducing Food

Introduce this theme by keeping a daily diary listing everything eaten. Classify the foods and graph the amounts. Compare the classification with the food pyramid (see *Me*, p. 119).

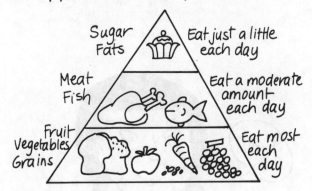

Make a pyramid and draw a record of one day's eating on it.
- Does it fit the model?
- Is the diet balanced?

Cultural Influences

Find out the cultural origins of foods eaten. Go back to the lists of food and classify according to country of origin. Extend the lists.

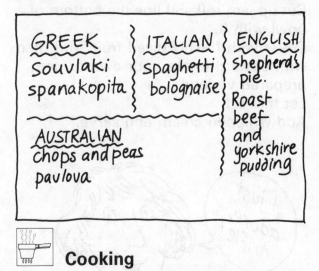

Cooking

Have an international lunch. (Every book on themes says this, we know! But have you ever done it?)
Menus for an international lunch

Menu 1:
- Irish stew
- English trifle

Menu 2:
- bean and bacon soup
- Malaysian satay
- tabouli

Menu 3:
- fried rice with meat and vegetable
- fruity roll

Menu 4:
- mini pizza
- carrot cake

Irish Stew

Fry onion and meat (lamb cut into small cubes) in some oil.
Add diced carrots, parsnips, potatoes and other root vegetables in season.
Add water and barley.
Bring to the boil, then turn heat down and simmer until cooked.

English Trifle

Cut up jam roll and line the bottom of a bowl with it.
Cover with freshly diced fruit, and then with custard (make your own or use prepared variety).
Let this set.
Add whipped cream and serve.

Fried Rice

The day before you cook fried rice, boil up enough rice for the recipe. When cooked, store in refrigerator until required.

Beat an egg. Fry it in a little peanut oil to make an omelette. Remove from pan and cut into strips.

Heat oil and fry diced meat (Chinese sausage or roast pork, bacon or ham) and some shrimps. Add chopped cabbage and bean shoots.
Add cold cooked rice and stir fry until heated through.
Sprinkle some (light) soy sauce and stir through.
Now add the omelette strips and chopped spring onion.
Mix and serve.

Excursion

Visit the local shops to survey those selling food. Include restaurants, fast food outlets, and supermarkets.
Talk to and watch the various food

workers. Compare fresh produce with processed food.

Word Study

List names given to different products which have the same base, for example:

rice	tomato
rice bubbles	tomato sauces
rice cakes	tinned tomatoes
'rice-a-riso'	spaghetti sauce
creamed rice	baked beans

Make a Food Mall
Children work in groups to make a shopping mall. Use cardboard boxes for construction.

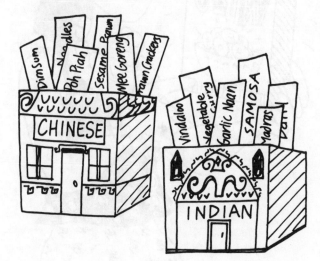

The 'shops' are used as word banks.

Reading

Read some stories about food:
- *Hansel and Gretel*, by Grimm Brothers
- *Stregga Nona* by Tomie de Paola
- *The Great Big Enormous Turnip* by Alexei Tolstoy
- *The Gingerbread Man*, traditional
- *Possum Magic* by Mem Fox
- *Stone Soup* by Mary O'Toole
- *How to eat Fried Worms* by Thomas Rockwell.

See *Bibliography* for details.

Art

Clay Food Sculptures
Make some food sculptures. Use clay to make a model of a favourite meal.

Still Life of Food
Look at still life paintings of food. Discuss the paintings. Children then paint their own still life paintings.

Printing with Food
Make some potato prints. Use carrot, broccoli, cauliflower and other vegetables to make prints, too.

Vegetable People Sculptures
Use toothpicks and a variety of fruit and vegetables to make sculptures of people.

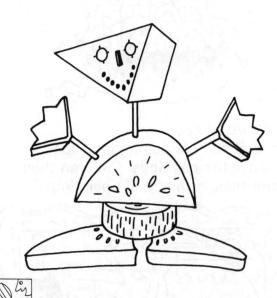

Research: Food Labelling

Collect food labels. Talk about the design of the labels, the use of colour, and so on which are used to market the product.

Which colours, names, labels are the most eye-catching and appealling? How much information is given about the food? Is it enough? What doesn't it tell you?

Design a Label
Design a label for a food product. It can be for an invented food. Draw it. Name it. List the contents. Tell how it is to be prepared. Describe what it tastes like. Design the packaging. Plan an advertising campaign. Make posters.

Give a cooking demonstration with your product. Present a television advertisement for your product.

Changing Foods

Change one food into another:
- pop corn in a frying pan
- make butter by shaking pure cream in a jar. Add a marble to the jar and it will happen faster. Use it on classroom-made bread rolls (see p. 71) and classroom-made jam.

Read *Jam* by Margaret Mahy and you'll find out how to make plum jam.

Old Food/New Food

Survey elderly people about the food that they ate when they were children. Ask about:
- types of food eaten
- availability
- where it was bought — shops, travelling vendors
- how often they ate certain foods
- how was food kept fresh?
- how was it stored?
- what cooking appliances were used?
- what was party food?
- what foods were served on special occasions?

Discussion

Food Related Health Issues
Find out and talk about:
- food poisoning
- anorexia
- malnutrition
- diabetes
- obesity
- tooth decay
- cancer
- food allergies
- starvation
- heart disease.

Food Chains
Find out about and discuss food chains.

Food Processing
Explore a variety of sequences.

 Growing Food
Grow some food. Try herbs to be used in classroom cooking or try growing beans, tomatoes, carrots, and other vegetables.

Visiting Speakers

Invite dieticians, food inspectors, a chef, and farmer or market gardener to speak to the class about their work.

 Word Study: Food Words

List words under the following categories.

People and food: for example, chef, orchardist, market gardener, pastry cook, vintner.

Places and food: for example, orchard, kitchen, restaurant, cafe, patisserie, farm, bakery, garden, hatchery, abattoir, cannery.

Preparation of food: for example, boil, bake, freeze, slice, dice, chop, fry, grill, stir, whip, beat,

Animals that provide food: for example, lamb, goat, deer, frog, snail, pigeon, fish eggs, shark, pig, chicken, rabbit, duckling.

Appliances used in food preparation: for example, blender, food processor, oven, microwave, toaster, fry pan, grill.

Foreign words used in cooking and about food: for example, saute, cafe, restaurant, pasta, legumes, zucchini, quiche.

Bread

Study bread and the variety of forms. Compare shapes, colour, texture and taste. On a map of the world label the origin of various breads.

Have an international bread tasting. Combine with cheese from different parts of the world. Invite parents to this cheese and bread tasting. Photograph the event. Prepare a class newspaper about the event, or prepare an article about the event for the class or school newspaper.

Bibliography

Aliki, *A Medieval Feast*, Bodley Head, 1984.

Armitage, Ronda, *The Lighthouse Keeper's Lunch*, Penguin, 1980.

Baldwin, Dorothy, *Your Body Fuel*, Wayland, 1983.

Bennett, Olivia, *Food for Life*, Macmillan, 1982.

Bosworth, Michael, *Food*, Methuen, 1983.

Cowley, Joy, *The Sausage Who Ate People*, Methuen, 1987.

Fox, Mem and Vivas, Julie, *Possum Magic*, Omnibus, 1987.

Grimm Brothers, *Hansell and Gretel*, Budget Books, 1985.

James, Frances, *Making Lunch*, Southern Cross, Macmillan, 1989.

Lester, Allison, *Clive Eats Alligators*, OUP, 1985.

Looking Back at Food and Drink, Macmillan, London, 1988.

Mahy, Margaret, *Jam*, Dent.

O'Toole, Mary, *Stone Soup*, Southern Cross, Macmillan, 1987.

Paterson, Libby and Sydenham, Shirley, *Your World: Food*, Southern Cross, Macmillan, 1987.

Rockwell, Thomas, *How to Eat Fried Worms*, Pan Books, 1979.

Sydenham, Shirley, *Let's Cook*, Southern Cross, Macmillan, 1989.

The Gingerbread Man, Traditional.

Thomas, Ron and Stutchbury, Jan, *Dairies*, Macmillan Beginners, Macmillan, 1988.

Thompson, Paul, *Nutrition*, Watts, 1981.

Tolstoy, Alexei and Oxenburg, Helen, *The Great Big Enormous Turnip*, Pan Books, 1972.

Vaughan, Marcia K., *Wombat Stew*, Ashton Scholastic, 1987.

Watson, Tom, *Breakfast*, Wayland, 1982.

Watson, Tom, *Evening Meal*, Wayland, 1982.

Watson, Tom, *Midday Meal*, Wayland, 1982.

Remembering

Introducing Remembering

Children bring photos from home of when they were younger. Talk about the photos, and about what they remember of the time when they were taken.

Bring photos of family members. Tell what they've been told about the times when these photos were taken.

Look at the photos and talk about the clothing fashions, hairstyles, furniture, transport, and so on.

Children find out about the origins of their family (try to start back with great-grandparents): build the family tree. From what countries did the family originate?

Write details of significant events in the family, for example: moving to a new house, a new country, or a different state; war; depression; change of jobs; winning a lottery.

Include photos, photocopies of memorabilia such as diaries, marriage certificates and birth certificates.

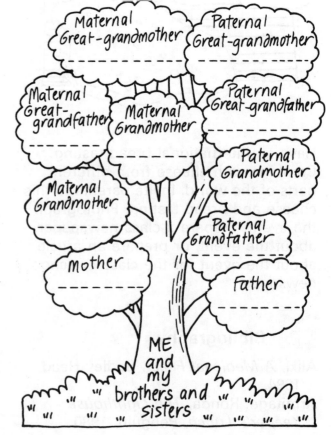

Early School Life

Talk about the early school life of the children:

- What are the things they remember?
- What things have changed?
- Are the changes good?

Collect their old school photos. Each child makes a personal timeline, from birth to the present day. Illustrate with photos and pictures.

Note memorable/significant events. Children interview parents for details of babyhood events and development.

Prepare a questionnaire for parents and grandparents. Record oral histories! Talk about all the history that gets lost because it is never recorded and kept.

Questions about parents' childhood:

- When and where were you born?
- How many brothers and sisters do you have?
- What school did you go to?
- How did you get to school?
- What occupations did your parents have?
- How old were you when you started school? Left school?

- Did you wear a school uniform?
- What was it like?
- What games did you play at school?
- What books did you read?
- What were the teachers like?
- How were children punished?
- How many children were there in your class? In your school?
- What did you take for lunch?
- What pets did you have?
- What jobs did you have to do at home?
- What sorts of things did you do on the weekends?
- What were your favourite toys?
- Did you get pocket money? How much?
- What did your family do in the evenings?

Questionnaire Results

Discuss the results of the questionnaire. Record statistical information by:

- graphing results where appropriate
- making charts
- making lists.

Whose parents		when born	where born	Brothers	Sisters
Kim	M	1951	Melb.	2	1
	D	1952	London	1	—
Jess	M	1958	Hong Kong	10	—
	D	1956	Beijing	2	4
Abdul	M	1960	Sydney	2	2
	D	1956	Lebanon	6	1
Sian	M	1948	Dublin	4	3
	D	1946	Melb.	2	4

Past Students
Invite past students to visit the school. Interview them and record the oral history, using questions above.
Also ask about the changes to the physical environment of the school and the neighbourhood. Look for old plans, maps and photos of the neighbourhood.

About the Neighbourhood
Ask the following questions about the neighbourhood.
- What is the origin of the name of your town or suburb?
- Who first lived in the area? Find out which group of Aborigines originally lived in the area. Contact an Aboriginal organisation (in your state, it could be through the Education Department) to find out the name of the group. Organise a guest speaker to visit and talk about the original inhabitants.
- When did the first European settlers come to the area?
- How did they treat the Aboriginal community?
- Was the area affected by the Gold Rush?
- Are there early monuments, and what do they record?
- What was the land used for in days of early settlement?
- When were the first schools built?

- Are they still there, and in use as schools?
- Was the area affected by World War I, World War II and the Depression? Find out about war industries, war service homes after the wars, people leaving the area.
- Recent changes and developments? Make maps of the area to show how it once looked and how it looks today. Walk around the neighbourhood to visit the sites where changes have been made or to sites of historical importance, such as the oldest house, or the first shop. Make a timeline of your town or suburb.

Research

Visit the local cemetery
Look at the headstones and read the inscriptions:
- Can we find out anything about problems and hardships of times past?
- Are some headstones more ornate than others?
- Are there family plots?

● Is it an old cemetery?

Take photos of the oldest gravestones. Make careful crayon rubbings of headstones. Record differences in spelling of words. Note the differences in inscription styles. Are these differences time related?

R.I.P.
John Stan
BORN
1907
DIED
1924

Changing Times

Look at transport, household appliances, furniture, fashions, and so on. Chart the developments through the years.

Look for old advertisements for these things. How much did they cost?

Visit the museum, pioneer settlements, historic houses, art gallery, railway museum to see these items.

Occupations

Find out about occupations which no longer exist, or which have changed over the years. Think about the jobs which exist today that may disappear in the future. Include occupations in the home as well as those outside.

Chimney Sweep

Games and Chants

From grandparents, parents, and other older people find out about favourite forms of common pastimes, such as marble games or skipping games played by people of different generations.

What chants can you collect from people of other generations and countries? Tape them.

Food

From grandparents, parents and other older people, find out about differences and similarities in foods and methods of preparation:

- utensils/appliances
- range and availability
- impact of other cultures
- restaurants and fast food chains.

Dress-up Day

Hold a dress-up day or an old-fashioned day. Children dress up as someone from their family profile (see previous activities) or in some appropriate 'old-fashioned' costume. Children can:

- write on slates, to do 'old-fashioned' schoolwork
- eat 'old-fashioned' food and play games of times past.

Time Capsule

Make and bury a time capsule so that children in the future can do a 'times past' theme. Children should suggest contents based on areas they have found particularly interesting or relevant:

- photos showing school uniforms, fashions
- pictures of cars, planes
- tickets from tram, train or bus
- school timetable
- watches
- recordings of latest music
- common toy or a toy computer game.

Drama: Video Time Capsule or Play

Based on their discoveries, discussions and conversations with old people, have groups prepare and present a 'video time capsule' of a specific era. They may like to incorporate anecdotes told to them about childhoods of long ago, mime old practices, and show the use of old-fashioned appliances such as those used for milking cows, separating cream, and churning butter. This presentation could be polished and presented to an audience of the people who were the source of information, or to a local elderly citizens' club or home. This could be a warm and enjoyable 'thank you' to round off the theme.

Bibliography

Black, J. Anderson, *A History of Fashion*, Orbis, 1982.

Durack, Mary, *Red Jack*, Southern Cross, Macmillan, 1987.

Flynn, Randal, *Digging up the Past*, Southern Cross, Macmillan, 1987.

Furniss, Elaine, and Abrahams, Hector, *31 Ferndale Street*, Southern Cross, Macmillan, 1989.

Herbert, Helen, *The Clothes they Wore*, CUP, 1986.

Kinnealy, Monica, *Number Please*, Southern Cross, Macmillan, 1989.

McKinlay, Brian, *Australia for Kids*, Collins Dove, 1987.

Mitchell, Greg, *Australian Lives*, Southern Cross, Macmillan, 1987.

Morrissey, David, *Ancient Australia*, A Children's History of Australia, Macmillan, 1986.

Odijk, Pam, *The Aborigines*, Ancient World, Macmillan, 1989.

Pearce, Margaret, *One day in the Life of a Maidservant*, Southern Cross, Macmillan, 1987.

Pigdon, Keith and Woolley, Marilyn, *Old Mr Hutton*, Southern Cross, Macmillan, 1987.

Stewart, Maureen, *Going Back in Time*, Southern Cross, Macmillan, 1987.

Wheatley, Nadia, *My Place*, Collins Dove, 1987.

Wignell, Edel, *Fiorella's Cameo*, Southern Cross, Macmillan 1987.

Wood, Darrelyn K, *Games with a Colonial Flavour*, D. K. Wood, 1986.

Shadows

Introducing Shadows

Outside, on a sunny day, begin the theme about shadows. Play shadow tiggy. Play it at different times of the day. Can the children decide which is the best time to play?

Maths

Tracing Shadows

Make shadows taller, smaller, wider, thinner. Trace around each other's shadows. Each child can make a shadow clock. With a partner, choose a spot in the yard, draw two footprints to mark where to stand each time a drawing is to be made. Every hour, the shadow is traced and the time recorded on it.

Measuring Shadows

Use a piece of string to measure the perimeter of your shadow.

Cast a shadow and cut it out. Make a 'flat stanley' kite. Write about yourself on the kite. Use it as writing paper and post a letter to someone.

Write a story about 'Me and my shadow'.

Read about Peter Pan losing his shadow, in *Peter Pan* by J.M. Barrie.

Shadow Magic

Try circus tricks with shadows.
Build a human pyramid, a human tower and so on. Use the paper shadows too.

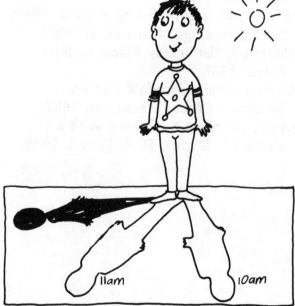

Can you make your shadow touch your partner without you actually touching? Try shaking hands, patting your partner's head, kissing.

Shadow Shapes
Set up a light source such as a projector and a screen (a wall or a sheet will do). Make the shadows move.

CAT:

straws for whiskers

hankie wrapped around wrist

COW:

BULLDOG:

Groups of children can make up a play using several of the shapes.
Photograph the shadows to enable the production of a story sequence. Or, use the photos to make a hand shadows book.

Making Silhouettes
Each child sits in front of the light source and their profile is traced. Cut out and stick onto contrasting paper.

Use the technique on an overhead projector to make silhouettes of other objects. They may be the real thing or a picture of the object. Make them as large or as small as you wish.

Puppets

Stick Puppets
Use the silhouettes to make stick puppets.

Make a shadow screen. You will need a blanket, a white sheet and a light source using a 100 watt pearl globe.

An alternate shadow screen can be made as shown in the illustration.

Shadow Marionettes
Make a shadow marionette.
The marionette can be 'dressed' and used as an ordinary marionette.

Make a shadow puppet with colour inserts.

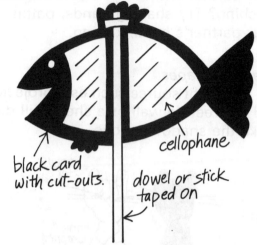

Scenery for your Shadow Play
Outline drawings of scenery can be taped to the screen. Coloured cellophane or tissue paper will give coloured scenery.

 Bibliography

Asch, Frank, *Bear Shadow*, Hodder and Stoughton, 1985.
Barrie, J.M., *Peter Pan*, Hodder, 1971.
Kuratomi, Chizuko, *Mr Bear's Shadow*, McDonald, 1980.

Snails

Introducing Snails

Begin this theme by looking for snails and collecting them. Look under stones, under leaves, in holes in walls, and in the letter box.

Read *Snail mail* by Hazel Edwards (see *Bibliography*).

While collecting the snails, observe and discuss the environment in which the snails were living:

- is it dry or wet?
- warm or cold?
- open or sheltered?
- what is growing nearby?
- what is the soil like?

 ## Science: Build a Snail Habitat

In the classroom build an enclosure for the snails.

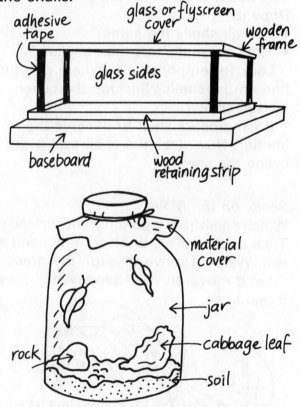

After spending some time observing the snails and discussing in groups, have the children label a snail diagram.

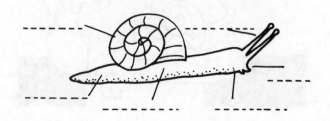

Focus observation on the snail's head:
- Can you find the mouth?
- Where are the eyes?
- What happens when you touch one of the long tentacles?
- What happens when you touch the other long tentacle?
- Does the snail react when a torch is shone on it?
- Does the snail react when you blow on it?

The Shell
Talk about the colour and pattern. Draw it.
- Are all shells the same?
- How do snails use their shells?

Look for empty shells. Where do you find empty shells? (Include the beach for sea snails).

Break open a shell to observe the interior. How does the snail seal itself inside the shell?

Snails on the Move
Watch snails move on different surfaces. Try a brick, a piece of glass, a tile, and a leaf. Watch it move through the grass.

Let it move on your hand. What does it feel like?

Watching Snails Eat
You can see its mouth and tongue with this experiment.

Make a paste of flour and water and spread it on a piece of glass. Look at the snail's mouth and tongue at work.

What will it Eat?
Overnight, leave small pieces of a variety of foods in the snailarium. In the morning talk about the snails' food preferences.

What will snails travel through? Draw or make circles around the snail with various substances, such as salt, vinegar, sugar, oil, cordial, and sand:
- Will it cross the circle?
- What does it do with its tentacles?

Snails' Ears?

Can snails hear? Clap your hands near the snail. Stamp your foot near it. What happens?

Research: Snail Reproduction

- How do snails breed?
- When do they hibernate?
- Snails that live in different places.
- Snails' enemies.

Writing: Spiral Snails

Draw some spirals. Write about a snail around the spiral.

Cut out the spiral and make a mobile snail poem or story.

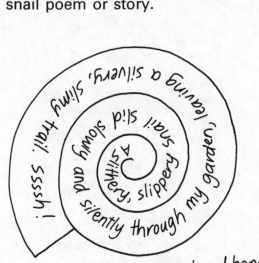

A slithery, slippery snail slid slowly and silently through my garden, leaving a silvery, slimy trail. sssss!

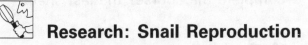

Cut out the spiral and hang...

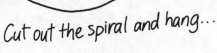

Snail Stamps

Make a snail stamp.

block of wood

string glued on

On a small block of wood, glue string or thick wool in the shape of a snail. When dry stamp onto paint soaked foam or a stamp pad, and then onto a piece of paper.

Snail Chain Stories

Write a chain story. Along a silvery trail (made with a felt pen on a long strip of paper) a group of children, in turn, write part of a snail's life story. The first child begins and writes for 2 minutes, the second reads the first child's writing and continues the story for 2 minutes and so on until all the children in the group have written.

Snail Sayings
Write down snail sayings:
- at a snail's pace
- slow as a snail

and so on. What do they mean?

Game: Snail Races

Mark snails' shells with coloured sticker dots and set up a racecourse for them. How long does it take: the first snail to complete the course? the last snail?

Bibliography

Edwards, Hazel, *Snail Mail*, Collins, 1988.
Hauptmann, Tatjana, *Adelina Schlime: A Snail Tale*, Benn, 1981.
Leonni, Leo, *The Biggest House in the World*, Anderson, 1978.
O'Hagan, Caroline, *It's Easy to have a Snail to Stay*, Chatto and Windus, 1980.

Spiders

Introducing Spiders

Be careful! Before commencing the hunt for spiders check with reference materials from the library to identify the dangerous spiders in your area. Leave them alone!

Funnel-web spider

Red-back spider

Spiders are best caught using a clear jar with a lid. Where to look:
- under leaves
- room corners
- under rocks
- between branches
- in the grass
- in holes in the ground
- among rubbish
- under bark
- on leaves
- on fences
- under the eaves
- along walls.

Prepare a chart which lists the places where spiders were found. Keep an on-going tally of sightings.

PLACE SIGHTED	NUMBER
Under the eaves	IIIII
In the corner of the classroom	IIIIII
In the playground	IIII

163

How to Keep Spiders

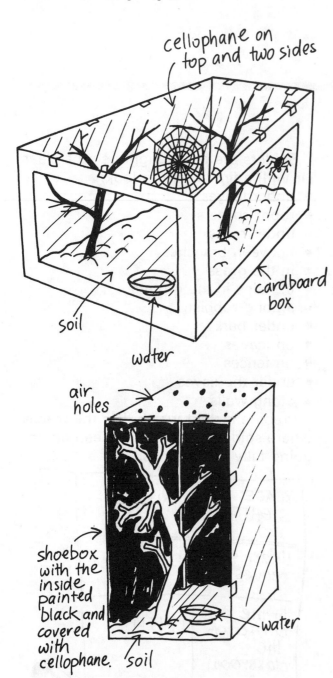

cellophane on top and two sides

cardboard box

soil

water

air holes

shoebox with the inside painted black and covered with cellophane.

water

soil

Catch flies and feed them to the spider:
- Will the spider eat a dead fly?
- How does the spider catch the fly?
- Will spiders eat other things? Try pieces of meat, caterpillars, snails, slaters, pieces of plant.

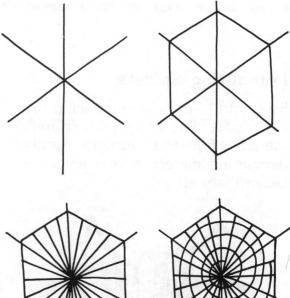

Research: Spiders' Webs

Do all spiders spin webs?
Some of those that do follow this pattern.

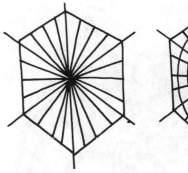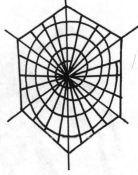

Use the pattern to make a giant web in a corner of the classroom. Make model spiders form papier-mache or from wax or clay and hang them in the web.

Make a flip book to show a spider building a web.

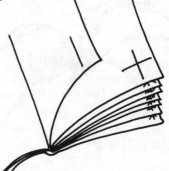

Look for other web styles. Make sketches of them. Which spiders live in them?

Trap a Spider's Web
Use spray enamel paint to lightly spray both sides of a spider's web. Hold a piece of paper against the wet web which should stick to the paper. Carefully cut the radials which are supporting the web. Lay the paper down to dry.

← radials →

Find out about:
- the most poisonous spiders in the world
- the largest and smallest spiders
- the life cycle of spiders
- distribution of spiders
- a spider's relatives.

Talk about the children's experiences with spiders. Why are people afraid of them? Talk about phobias.

SPIDER!

Observing Spiders

Observe the spiders. Compare length, size, markings, colours, and shapes.
How do the spiders respond to:
- noise (clap near them)
- light (shine a torch on them)
- movement (touch the web lightly with a stick).

Spider Songs
Sing the song 'There was an old woman who swallowed a fly' (see *Bibliography*).

Make a model of the old lady and all the things that she swallowed. Use when retelling the story of the song.

Classifying Spiders

Classify spiders into web spinning and non-web spinning. Find pictures of them. Make charts. Children can present their research work in book form.

Bibliography

Appiah, Peggy, *Tales of an Ashanti Father*, Deutsch, 1967.

Back, Christine, *Spider's Web*, Black, 1984.

Baker, Jeannie, *One Hungry Spider*, Ashton Scholastic, 1988.

Carle, Eric, *The Very Busy Spider*, Hamish Hamilton, 1985.

Graham, Margaret Bloy, *Be Nice to Spiders*, World's Work, 1969.

Lane, Margaret, *The Spider*, Collins.

'There was an old woman who swallowed a fly,' in *Boa Constrictor and other Crushing Poems*, Southern Cross, 1987.

Wagner, Jenny, *Aranea*, Penguin, 1975.

White, E.B., *Charlotte's Web*, Macmillan Books, 1981.

Williams, Ursula Moray, *Spid*, Andersen, 1985.

A spider mobile

← information cards →

Trees

Introducing Trees

To begin this theme go for a walk around the neighbourhood to get to know the trees. Classify them in terms of size, shape, shape of leaves, thickness of trunk, and texture of trunk. Graph the species according to average heights.

Investigate the ground under the tree. What has fallen from the tree? Look for leaves, seeds, flowers, fruit, bark...any dead birds?

Begin a leaf collection.

Measuring Trees
Measure the distance around the trunk.
- Hug the tree — can you reach around it?

- Use a piece of string to measure and compare the circumferences of other trees.
- Walk around the tree, heel-to-toe — how far is it using this measurement?

Use forestry workers' trick of estimating a tree's height: with arm outstretched, hold a stick upright, lined up with the tree, and adjust the stick until it seems to be the same height as the tree. Now pivot the stick downwards so it is at a right angle to the tree and note where the end is parallel along the ground line. This distance can be measured to give a rough idea of the trees height.

height of tree

Research

Tree Names
Use an identification book to find out the names of the trees.

Find out and list the differences between deciduous and evergreen trees. Record this information on classroom charts.

TREE	NAME	SHEDS LEAVES IN AUTUMN/ WINTER	EVERGREEN
🌲	Pine		✓
🌳	Gum		✓
🌳	Oak	✓	

Seasonal Changes
Take a photo of a tree or draw a sketch. Then in a few months, go back and observe the seasonal changes. If the tree is deciduous the seasonal observation could be done at least 4 times in a year.

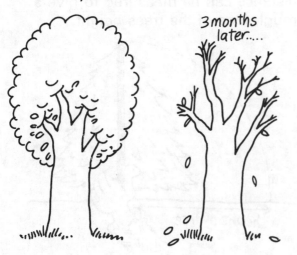

A Tree as a Home
On a large chart show all of the animals which make their homes in or near a tree.

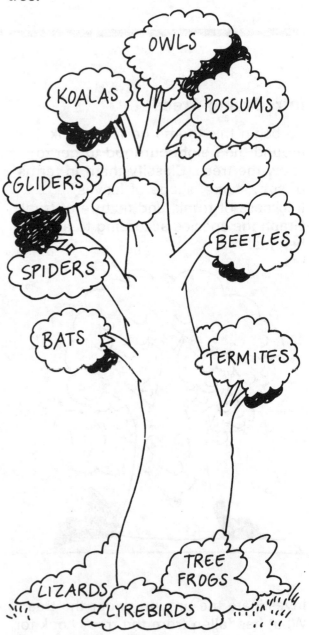

Root Systems
Talk about the root system and the function of the roots:
● to gather food
● to anchor the tree
● tap root
● root hairs.

Be a Tree Detective

One child leads a blindfolded partner to a tree. The blindfolded one uses all their senses (except sight) to explore the tree. Touch the bark, hug it, smell it and listen to it.

The blindfolded person is then led away from the tree. When the blindfold is removed, can the person who was blindfolded find his or her tree?

Trees That Give Us Food

Find out and list trees that we get food from. For example, walnut, almond, pear, apple, and so on. Find pictures of them. Make a zig-zag folder of food trees.

How Trees Help People

Find out and discuss how trees help people:
- clean the air
- stop erosion and salinity
- wind breaks
- shade
- timber
- paper making
- food.

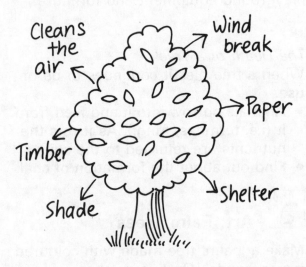

The Timber Industry

Find out about the timber industry. Debate the issues of woodchipping and logging our forests:
- What are the dangers of too much logging?
- What is happening to the world's forests?

Which countries have forest industries? Locate them on a world map.

Forest Workers

How do they care for the forest? How can we help care for the forest? Talk about the effects of pollution, bushfires, clearfelling, grazing animals and feral animals.

Visit a forest and talk to a forestry worker.

Other Tree Products
Find out about other products from trees:
- rubber
- maple syrup
- oils
- paper.

Find out about things made of wood. Collect pictures of timber products, such as houses, fences, gates, playground equipment and furniture.

The Death of a Tree
When a tree dies it continues to be of use.
- Animals burrow into it and feed from it (i.e. termites, fungi). As it rots the nutrients are returned to the soil.
- Find out about the formation of coal.

Art: Palm Trees

Make a 'palm' tree made with coloured paper 'hands'. On a large sheet of paper, draw a trunk for the tree. Have the children trace around their hand onto coloured paper. Cut out the shapes. Paste the hand at the wrist, fingers down, onto the tree to form the leaves.

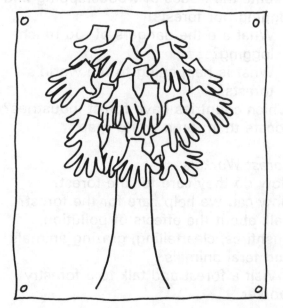

Rubbings
Make a bark rubbing.

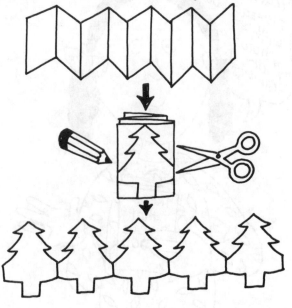

Collage
Use the bark, leaves, seed pods and seeds to make a collage of a tree, or if you're adventurous, a forest.

A String of Trees
Concertina fold the paper, draw the tree shape. Cut around the shape.

Word Study

Build words using tree words:

- arbor, aboreal, arboreous, aboretum
- log, logging, logger
  log book, log cabin, log canoe
- wood, wooden, woody, wooded
  wood carver, woodcraft, wood-cutter
  wood shed, woodland, wood pecker

Other words to try:

- branch
- grow
- plant
- seeds
- sap.

Word Trees
Write about trees to make word trees.

Trees give us shelter, food, shade, places for cubbies, things to climb, beauty, clean air, healthy soil, flowers and fragrance

Guest Speaker

Furniture Maker
Invite a furniture maker to talk to the class about his or her craft.

Look back at the development of furniture. Find out about the use of wood to build ships, carriages and other modes of transport.

Carpenters
Talk about:

- the work of a carpenter
- the tools used by a carpenter.

Papermaking

Materials needed:
electric blender
picture frame (no larger than 20×25 cm) with flyscreen stapled on
a stack of newspapers
a large, deep container larger than the frame
2 white desk blotters
a wooden spoon
paper towelling
an iron

Materials for making the pulp:
junk mail
magazines
wrapping paper
newsprint

You can use a larger quantity of a particular colour, for example, lots of red will give you pinkish paper.

1. Tear the paper into strips and loosely pack into blender until 1/3 full. Add water until blender is 2/3 full, and blend for 5 seconds. Add more strips of predominant colour and blend again. Texture can be added at this point, such as parsley sprigs, grasses, flowers, fabric fibres.

2. Make 3 piles of newspapers: the first with the container on it. Place a sheet of blotting paper on the second. Empty the blender contents into the container, and add water to a depth of 3 or 4 centimetres, stirring well. Angle the frame, screen side up, and spoon mixture evenly over the screen. Hold this over the container to let excess water drip off.

3. Working quickly, place long edge of frame on the blotter and flip over, mush side down. Use paper towelling to soak up moisture seeping through screen, especially at edges.

4. Carefully lift off frame, and cover the wet paper with the other blotter. Move this sandwich to third pile of newspapers, and iron both sides, on 'wool' setting. Remove the top blotter and peel off the paper. If it doesn't come off easily it isn't dry enough: iron the paper directly until it does peel off easily.

Build Paper Cubbies

Children roll up sheets of newspaper to form tubes. This can be done by rolling the pages around pieces of dowelling, which are then removed. The rolls are secured with sticky tape or masking tape at each end. These tubes form the framework of the cubby; sheets of newspaper stuck in place form the walls. This can be a group activity, with each group having to design their own cubby, which must be large enough to house the entire group at once, seated on cushions. A window can be stipulated as one of the conditions.

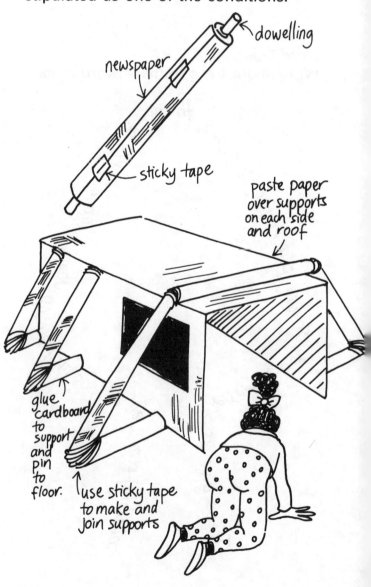

newspaper

dowelling

sticky tape

paste paper over supports on each side and roof

glue cardboard to support and pin to floor.

use sticky tape to make and join supports

Geodesic Domes

Alternatively, as a whole class cooperative task, a geodesic dome can be made. The rolls of newspaper are made again, but must be a standard size (for example, tabloid pages rolled from the shorter edge). They are taped together to form triangles. The triangles are joined together with tape and a dome shape is formed. The triangles have paper pasted over them, some covered with wrapping paper or newsprint, and some with coloured cellophane.

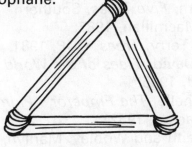

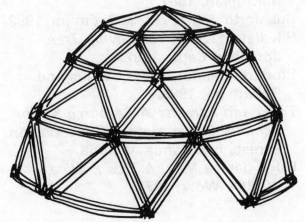

Plant Your Own Trees

Collect seeds from underneath trees and try to grow them. Extract the seed from the seed pod and plant in a container or in a plastic bag to germinate.

Plant in the soil in spring.
Keep it well-watered and watch it grow.

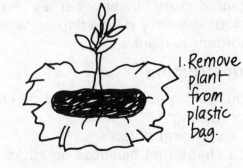

1. Remove plant from plastic bag.

2. Loosen the roots

3. Plant, and press soil firmly around the base.

Making Natural Dyes

Collect leaves (you will need double the weight of the material to be dyed). Put the leaves in an enamel or stainless steel saucepan. Add water to just cover the leaves. Simmer for one hour. Strain to remove the leaves.

A mordant is added to this liquid to help 'fix' the dye to the material. The most common mordants are alum or chrome:

Alum — 60 grams for each half kilogram of material.

Chrome (potassium dichromate) — use 10 grams for each half kilogram of material.

Place the dampened material into the dye and simmer for about half an hour. Rinse the dyed material in cold running water until it rinses clear. Dry away from direct sunlight.

Leaves to try: cootamundra wattle, silver wattle, river red gum, lemon scented gum, lilly pilly berries — the colour will vary depending on which mordant is used.

Construction

Construct objects with wood off-cuts. Try making:

- a standing object
- a shape that balances on sticks
- a useful object
- a moving object
- a wearable object.

Build a Tree House

Bibliography

Boulton, Carolyn, *Trees*, Watts, 1984.

Burnie, David, *Tree*, Collins, 1988.

Dodd, Lynley, *The Apple*, Keystone, 1982.

Edwards, Ian, *Trees for Kids*, Collins Dove, 1988.

Greenwood, Ted, *VIP: Very Important Plant*, Angus and Robertson, 1971.

Hathorn, Elizabeth, *Stephen's Tree*, Methuen, 1979.

Hogan, Paula Z., *The Oak Tree*, Raintree, 1979.

Howes, Jim, *Five Trees*, Southern Cross, Macmillan, 1987.

Jennings, Terry, *Trees*, OUP, 1981.

Lambert, David, *Trees of the World*, Wayland, 1985.

Nikly, Michelle, *The Emperor's Plum Tree*, Macrae, 1982.

Pigdon, Keith and Wooley, Marilyn, *River Red*, Southern Cross, Macmillan, 1987.

Rushforth, Keith, *Trees*, Optimum, 1983.

Silverstein, Shel, *The Giving Tree*, Jonathan Cape, 1987.

Stodart, Eleanor, *Trees*, Angus and Robertson, 1983.

Trees and Forests: A Resource Kit for Schools, Department of Conservation, Forests and Lands, Victoria,

Udry, Janice May, *A Tree is Nice*, World's Work, 1971.

Under Umbrellas

Introducing Umbrellas

Make a collection of umbrellas. Classify them in different ways: according to colour, shape, size, use, culture.

Wet Day Activities

Kim's Game

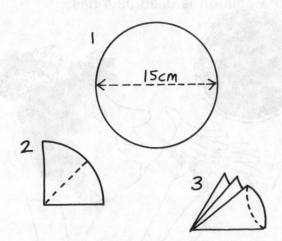

1

15cm

2

3

4

5

Make umbrellas.
Use the umbrellas to play 'Kim's Game'. Stick magazine pictures or draw pictures on the umbrella. Children swap umbrellas with each other, study the pictures for a given length of time, hide the umbrella and write down all the items they can remember.

Indoor Tabloid Sports

- Bean Bags in the Bin
  A wastepaper bin is set up and from a designated distance each child, in turn, tries to throw a bean bag into the bin. Scoring: 2 points for each bean bag in the bin.

- Walking Along a Line
  Mark a 3 metre line on the floor. In turn, each child must walk along the line and back with a book balanced on his or her head. Scoring: 10 points is allocated to each child at the

start of his or her turn, and 2 points are deducted each time the book is dropped.

- **Ball Rolling**
Along a marked course, children push a ball using only their heads. The circuit could be the rest of that group, standing in a previously designated formation. Scoring: 5 points for each completed circuit.
- **Bowling**
Set up 10 plastic bottles at the end of an aisle. Using a soft rubber or plastic ball, each child in turn rolls the ball to see how many bottles he or she can knock down. They are re-set after each turn. Scoring: 1 point for each bottle knocked down, 10 for each 'strike', that is when all 10 are knocked down. All points are added together for a team score rather than individual scores.

- **An Obstacle Course**
Make a short obstacle course: under a table, over a chair, through a hoop, crawling across the platform and between two blocks, 'limbo' under a stick placed across two objects, and so on. In turn, children complete the course without knocking down the obstacles. Scoring: 5 points for each completed circuit.
Rotate the groups around the 5 activities, totalling the cumulative scores for each group.

Balloon Volleyball
Children remain seated for this game, and a balloon is used as a ball.

Paper Plane Contest
Children make paper planes using any designs they wish. (See p. 56)

A target is set up: a broadsheet newspaper page with a hole cut in the centre is hung up. From a given mark, children try to fly their planes through the hole. A scoring system can be devised, using criteria like speed, height, consistency and smoothness of flight, as well as points for going through the hole. Landing distance from the hole can also be taken into account.

Drama: Surviving Floods

Talk about floods: the damage, the causes and effects, how people cope in a crisis, helping each other, and so on. Perhaps anecdotes will emerge.

Children form themselves into families: leave the structure and roles up to each group to decide. Encourage a variety of family structures and age groups. All roles must be people; not animals.

When they have organised their roles, each 'family' finds a space in the room which will be their home in a small village. Discuss what their homes are like and what their tasks and occupations are.

Allow time for the families to go about their day's tasks, enacting their roles. When they have had time to enrole, have them prepare a series of 'photographs' depicting each member of the family employed in a typical task, while another member introduces that person.

Now let village life take its course, with all the families interacting, as a picture of that village comes to life. The teacher can participate in the role of mayor, instituting the custom of the village warning bell that summons all the village to the square in an emergency. Begin talking about the rain, and will it ever stop, begin to be concerned at the rising river higher up the mountain. The children should catch on and begin to voice their concerns too.

Call a village meeting. The situation is looking grave, and the river is higher than ever before in history. The villagers must suggest courses of action such as sandbagging, and moving precious things to the Town Hall's second storey. They then go about these tasks. People will react in character, for example an elderly woman and man will ask for help in moving their belongings, and so on. What things are essential to be saved?

When they are asleep in their homes, ring the alarm bell. The river has broken its banks and the floods are raging into the village. The teacher is still in role, getting things moving. The villagers all rush somehow to the safety of the Town Hall (the highest spot), battling the swirling torrents, and all the debris that is being swept along. Urge them to help each other, express concern for weak/missing/elderly people.

The next scene is after the flood waters have subsided. Tell the villagers to return to their homes to assess the damage, salvage what they can, and to begin cleaning up.

When they are doing this, the teacher changes roles to become a television news reporter. Visit each home in turn and ask what the damage is, what has been lost and saved, was anyone injured or lost, and so on. Keep it moving briskly so that they retain role commitment.

In turn, each family group will present another series of 'photographs' that tell about the effect on their family of the flood, what they lost and what they saved.

End with a reflection time to talk about crisis, people's reactions, the feelings involved in losing belongings or loved ones through catastrophe, what becomes valuable when you can only save a few things, and so on.

After the Drama Lesson
Write in role about the flood:
- the journalist
- the old person
- a child
- a rescue worker
- a mother.
Read about the Great Flood!

 Research

Umbrellas are also used on the beach and to protect us from the sun! Discuss these other ways that umbrellas offer protection.

 Art

Umbrella Mobiles
Make mobiles using umbrella frames for bases.

Other mobiles to try on a wet day:

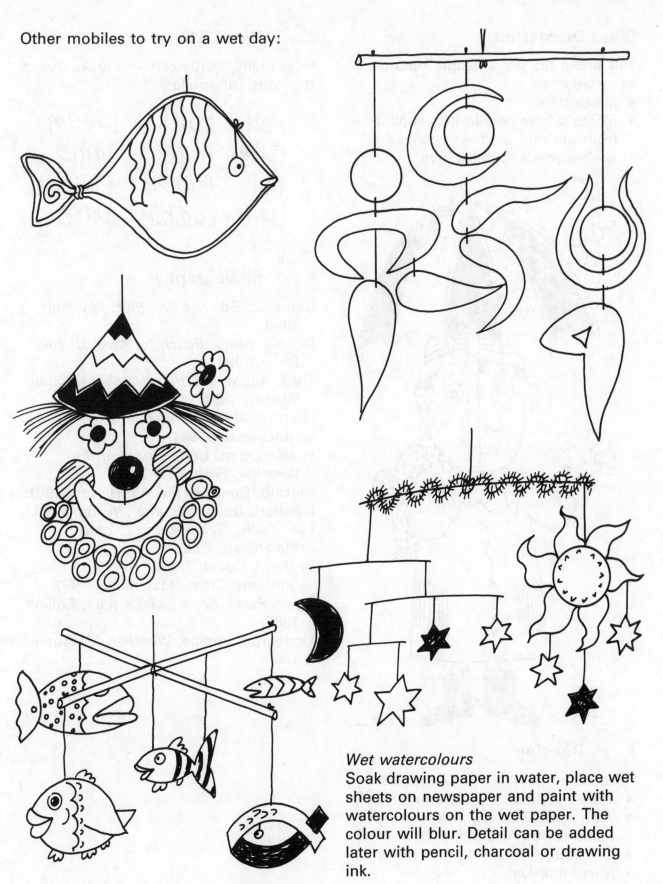

Wet watercolours
Soak drawing paper in water, place wet sheets on newspaper and paint with watercolours on the wet paper. The colour will blur. Detail can be added later with pencil, charcoal or drawing ink.

Class Discussion

Talk about the ways people keep dry in rainy weather:
- rainclothes
- places where people take shelter from the rain, such as verandahs, shelter sheds, bus shelters.

Reading

Read about people with umbrellas.
- *Mary Poppins* (or watch the video!)
- *John Had Great Big Waterproof Boots On* by A.A. Milne
- *Christopher Robin* by A.A. Milne
- *Nurse Matilda*.

 Word Study

How many words can you make out of the word 'umbrella'?

red   ball   bream
rub   mare   lamb
bull   marble   meal
bell   rumble   bare

Bibliography

Catherall, Ed, *The Weather*, Wayland, 1986.

Dracup, Mary, *Beach for Kids*, Collins Dove, 1988.

Ford, Adam, *Weather Watch*, Methuen/ Walker, 1981.

Gerrard, Jean, *Matilda Jane*, Hutchinson, 1981.

Hudson, Jim, *Understanding the Weather*, Globe, 1982.

Kincaid, Doug, *In the Air*, Hulton, 1981.

Lambert, David, *Weather*, Watts, 1983.

Lye, Keith, *Weather and Climate*, Macmillan, 1983.

Pearson, David, *The Umbrella*, Southern Cross, Macmillan, 1987.

Spier, Peter, *Peter Spier's Rain*, Collins, 1982.

Updegraff, Imelda, *Weather*, Methuen, 1980.

Volts

Introducing Batteries

Children bring to school any battery-operated toys and appliances. Observe these in action:

- What parts move?
- How are they joined?
- Where does the wiring go?
- How many batteries are needed?
- Where are they housed?
- How are they placed?

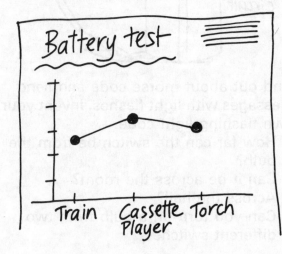

Testing Batteries
Using new batteries, test to see how long they will run a selection of toys continuously.

Battery test

Train   Cassette   Torch
        Player

Experiment

Lighting up Bulbs
Each child is given a battery, a small torch bulb and a piece of copper wire. How many children can get the bulb to light up? Are there different ways of doing it successfully?

Compare and discuss the different methods, and the reasons for the success or failure of different methods.

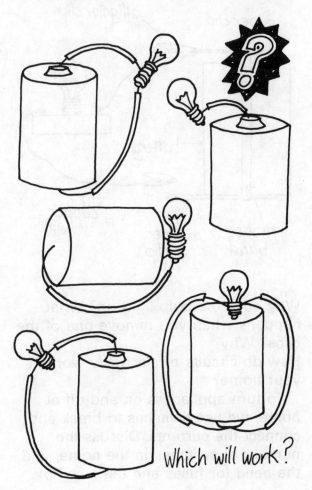

Which will work?

Make a Bulb Holder
Use a purchased bulb holder (at electrical supply shops) or make them, as illustrated.

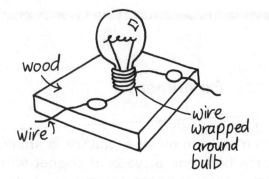

Making Switches
Make a switch as shown.

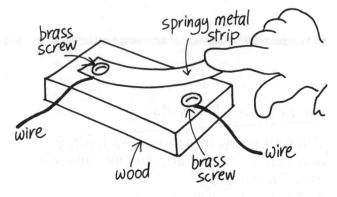

Making and Breaking Circuits

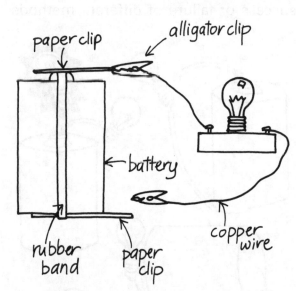

Why does the bulb light up? What happens when you remove one of the clips? Why?
How do circuits of electricity work in your home?
   To turn appliances on and off at home, we use switches to break and connect the currents. Discuss the number of switches in the home, and the need for fuses and the fuse box.

Make a circuit with a switch

Find out about morse code and send messages with light flashes. Invent your own flashing light code.
- How far can the switch be from the bulb?
- Can it be across the room?
- Across the hall?
- Can you turn on a bulb from two different switches?

Discuss: how many switches does a two-way circuit like that at home have? Make a circuit with two switches as illustrated.

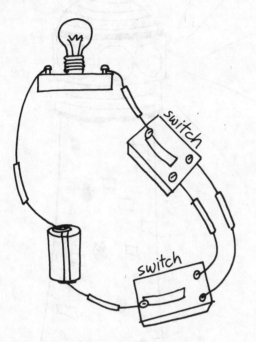

Lighting More Than One Bulb
Can you light up more than one bulb on a circuit? Try.

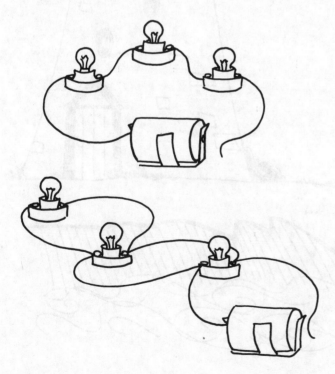

Joining Cells
Can you join several cells to light the bulb? Does the light shine brighter? Does the light last longer?

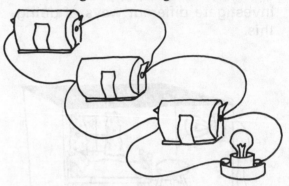

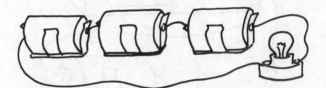

Investigate the workings of a torch.

 Make a Doorbell

Using a purchased doorbell mechanism, children make a circuit as above to make the bell ring when the switch is connected.

183

Use the knowledge acquired in previous experiments to:

- light a dolls' house or a model theatre (or finger puppet theatre). Investigate different ways of doing this.

- Make a lighthouse that lights up.

- Try making a robot out of scrap materials, and giving it flashing eyes.

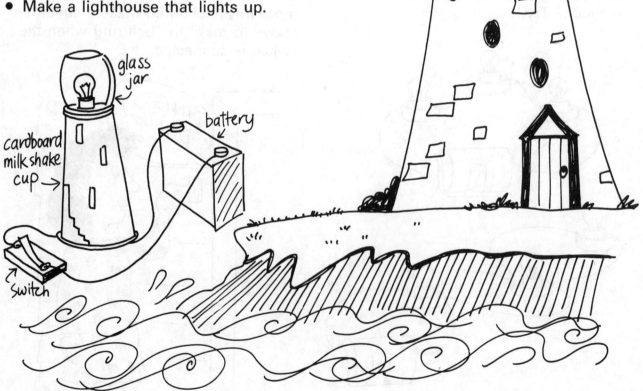

Research: Electricity

Find out about:
- people who made major discoveries and inventions in the field of electricity
- uses of electricity in industry and at home. What would our lives be like without it?
- how is electricity generated?
- how does it get across the country?

Electricity Safety

Launch a schoolwide safety campaign to promote using electricity safely. Make posters.

Bibliography

Ardley, Neil, *Discovering Electricity*, Watts, 1984.

Bailey, Mark W., *Electricity*, Raintree, 1978.

Catherall, Ed, *Electric Power*, Wayland, 1981.

Jennings, Terry, *Electricity and Magnetism*, OUP, 1982.

Life would be so different without ELECTRICITY!

Water

Introducing Water

Build a mountain of soil, approximately 1 metre high in the school yard. Each child will decorate and label an icy pole stick and insert it in the mountain.

Prop a hose in a position so that it can 'rain' on the mountain.

After the 'rain' has been falling for several minutes, erosion will occur, and can be seen in the following features:
- valley
- stream
- waterfall
- fan
- delta
- dam.

The children will also note the position of their sticks.

Take photographs throughout the experiment. Use the photos to compile an illustrated report.

Experiment

Another experiment to show the effects of water on the land: fill 2 shoe boxes with soil. Seed one of the boxes with grass seed. Let it sprout. When sprouted, put lots of leafy twigs to simulate forest vegetation.

Fill a second box with soil. When water is 'rained' onto the boxes the children will observe the results. Discuss and draw conclusions.

Research the use of rain gauges by meteorologists. What other measurements of precipitation are made? Collect and discuss daily precipitation contour maps.

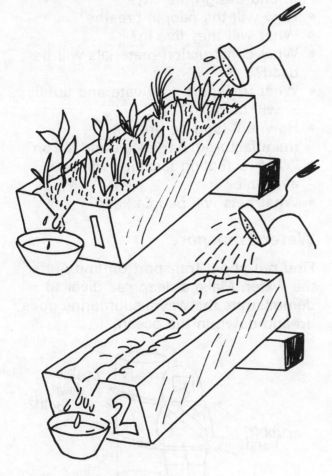

Evaporation

Evaporation
After rain (or make your own rain), draw lines around several puddles on the asphalt.

Every hour, redraw the lines around the puddles. Note the rate of evaporation.
Where has the water gone?

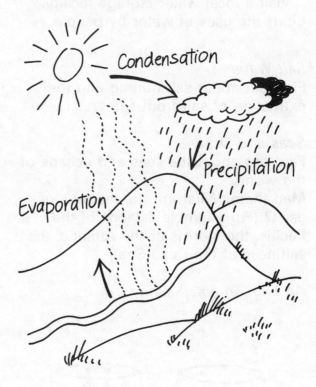

Make Rain Gauges
Measure the rainfall using one of the following rain gauges.

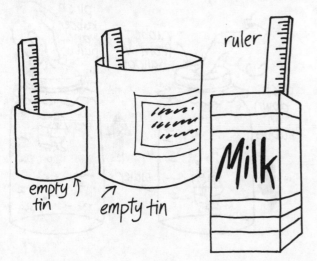

Other Evaporation Experiments
Place several saucers of water on a sunny ledge. Each saucer of water will have the same quantity of water but will have an additive, such as salt, sugar, soil, cordial, food dye, and so on.

Time and measure the rate of evaporation. Do the additives make a difference? What is left in the saucers when the water has gone?

 **Research**

Find out about:
- the storage of water for domestic use – in a city? on a farm?
- the distribution of stored water to houses
- how the water supply is kept clean
- the people who work at the jobs involved with the water supply.
  Visit a local water storage facility.
Chart the uses of water by people.

Salt Water
Find out about salt mining and the extraction of salt from sea water.

Seas and Oceans
Find out about the seas and oceans of the world.
Map them. What are the features of each? (For example, islands of the Pacific, the storms of the Atlantic, the saltiness of the Dead Sea.)

An Experiment: Salinity

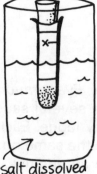

Underwater Cities

Find out and read about Atlantis.
Talk about living in an underwater city.
Plan and design the city:
- How will the people breathe?
- What will they live in?
- What construction materials will be used?
- What transport – private and public – will be used?
- How will food be grown, manufactured, harvested and so on?
- What recreation facilities will be available?
- What pets will people keep?

Water Transport

Find out about transport on and under the water. Make a deep sea diver to demonstrate the way a submarine goes up and down in the ocean.

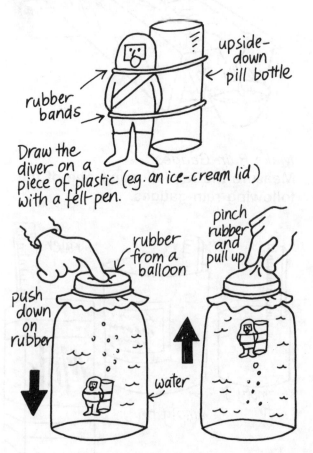

Early Sailing Vessels
Make models of early sailing vessels.
Test to see if they will float.

The Plimsoll Line
Find out about the Plimsoll line.
● What is it?
● Origin – who was it named after?
(The Plimsoll line is a line or mark that must be placed on the hull of all British merchant vessels to show the depth to which they may be submerged through loading. The Plimsoll line was named after Samuel Plimsoll, a politician and social reformer, who lived from 1824 to 1898.)

 ## Water Sports

Find out about water recreations.
Make a book about:
● swimming
● sailing
● water skiing
● sailing
● diving
● fishing
● surfing
● scuba diving
● canoeing
● rowing
and so on.

Making a Book

Sew the pages together 6mm from the spine

THE COVER:

1. Cut 2 pieces of cardboard slightly larger than the pages, and a thin spine.

2. Cut wallpaper, cover paper or material to cover the card.

3. Glue the cards and spine onto the paper.

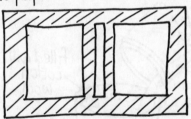

4. Put glue on remaining material and fold edges over.

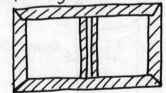

5. Insert the pages.

 ## Writing

Use the following starters to write about water.
● The day the school was flooded.
● The day it rained cats and dogs.
● 'Water, water everywhere and never a drop to drink.'

Water Words

Aqua is the Latin word for water.
Find words with aqua in them:

aquaphobia	aquamarine
aquarium	aqualung
aquarelle	aquatic
aquaduct	aquanaut

Make a list of water words:

waterwheel	waterbed
water-beetle	waterdrop
waterbird	water barrel
water-buffalo	waterfall

Water Works

Make a water filter.

Make a waterwheel.
Use heavy duty foil from the inside of a powdered milk or coffe tin. Cut and fold as shown in the following diagram.

Can the children think of a way that the power of the waterwheel can be harnessed to work for them?

Observing Pond Life
Set up an aquarium to observe pond life.

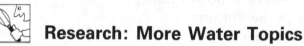

Research: More Water Topics

Find out about:
- how were waterwheels used in the past?
- why aren't they used as much now?
- hydro-electricity
- the great dams of the world
- fountains
- plants that grow in the water
- animal life in water.

Other topics for investigation:
- mammals that live in the water
- waterbirds
- marine biology
- insects that breed in the water
- exploration of the sea
- extraction of the fuel from under the sea
- seaweed and other food sources found in water
- coral atolls
- fishing industry.

Art

Tie Dyeing

1. Clean fabric

2. Bunch it together with rubber bands.

3. Dip into colour.

4. Hang on the line to dry.

5. Untie.

Dip Dyeing

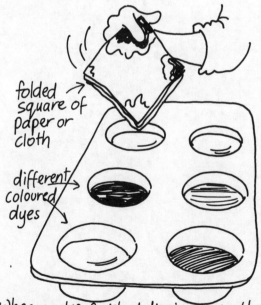

folded square of paper or cloth

different coloured dyes

When you've finished dipping, press the folded paper between newspaper to squeeze out the extra dye, then open it up and leave it to dry.

Marbling

In a container, mix oil-based paint and turpentine. Use a different container for each colour used.

Using a container which is larger than the paper size being used (for example a baking dish) half fill it with water.

Add two or three of the mixed colours. Swirl them into interesting patterns. Float a piece of paper on the surface. Lay the paper flat to dry.

Use your marbled paper as wrapping paper, book covering, endpapers for homemade books, and so on.

191

Bibliography

Ardley, Neil, *Working with Water*, Watts, 1983.

Coleridge, Ann, *Longneck's Billabong*, Southern Cross (Big Book and Reader), Macmillan, 1987.

Dineen, Jacqueline, *Rivers and Lakes*, The Face of the Earth, Macmillan, London, 1987.

Dugan, Michael, *Water*, Macmillan, 1981.

Exploring Rivers, Pathfinders in Exploration, Macmillan, 1987.

Exploring the Oceans, Pathfinders in Exploration, Macmillan, 1987.

Fox, Julian, *The Water from Your Tap*, Wayland, 1982.

Gordon-Smith, Catherine, *From Rain to Tap*, Globe Education, 1981.

Houghton, G. and Wakefield, J., *The Coast and the Sea*, Living in Australia, Macmillan, 1990.

Houghton, G. and Wakefield, J., *Water, Soil and Air*, Living in Australia, Macmillan, 1990.

Howes, Jim, *Down, Roundabout and Up Again: The Life of a River*, Southern Cross, Macmillan, 1987. (Big Book and Reader)

Hutchins, Pat, *The House that Sailed Away*, Armada books, 1978.

Hutton, Deane, *Water*, Jacaranda, 1980.

Jennings, Terry, *Floating and Sinking*, OUP, 1988.

Jennings, Terry, *Water*, OUP, 1982.

Lewis, Alun, *Water*, Watts, 1980.

Pigdon, Keith and Woolley, Marilyn, *River Red*, Southern Cross, Macmillan, 1987.

Porter, Keith, *Life in the Water*, The Animal Kingdom, Macmillan, 1986.

Satchwell, John, *Water*, Watts, 1985.

The Book of Water, Benn, 1980.

Thomas, Ron and Stutchbury, Jan, *Weather*, Macmillan Beginners Science, Macmillan, 1989.

Tuffin, Bruce (Ed.), *Your World: The Sea*, Southern Cross, Macmillan, 1987.

Witches

Introducing Witches

Read a selection of stories from the bibliography, to begin this theme. Choose some that are about good witches, and some that are about bad witches.

Classify the characteristics of the witches into:

- good
- bad
- things common to both.

Talk about what witches look like. Discuss all types from the stereotypical hook-nosed, all in black, all evil, warty and gnarled to the modern, like everyone else, helpful witch.

Paint a picture for a classroom gallery of witches.

Modern Witches

Design an outfit for a modern day witch.

Update witches' transport. Brooms are too slow; what do they use now?

A cauldron is an inefficient cooking utensil; what would a modern witch use?

A witch always had a familiar (pet helper, often a cat). Give your modern witch a trendy, up-to-date familiar.

Design a modern witch supermarket. What products would it sell? What would the 'black spot specials' be? What would the 'broom park' be like?

Drama

Read *Suppose You Met a Witch*, by Ian Serrailler (see *Bibliography*).

Children move around the room as the witch. The teacher or a child casts spells to turn the rest of the class into a rapid succession of creatures, such as a frog, duck, snake, insect, caterpillar and so on.

He or she then casts spells which turn them into a variety of humans engaged in a variety of occupations such as a one-armed juggler, a clown whose feet are glued to the floor, a baker kneading some dough that keeps rising and increasing in volume, an assembly line worker trying to keep up with a task when the assembly line keeps increasing in speed, and so on.

In pairs, the children tell each other's fortunes, by palm-reading or gazing into an imaginary crystal ball.

Invent a spell recipe, and write it down. The children must make up a chant to go with the cooking up of the spell, and enact the whole process. As the final potion is being ladled out, they must say what the spell will do to the person who drinks it (or eats it, rubs it on, smells it, sees it, whatever!)

In groups of four or five, children work out and present an 'essence' of a haunted house. Each group member thinks of one movement and an associated sound. These are presented one after the other, in rapid succession. Members are 'frozen' before and after their movement.

I can't move!

List and discuss superstitions:
- keeping a horseshoe
- walking under a ladder
- a black cat crosses your path
- touching wood
- keeping a rabbit's foot
- spilling salt
- number 13 or lucky 7
- four-leaf clover
- opening an umbrella inside the house
- putting new shoes on the table
- breaking a mirror brings seven years bad luck
- stepping on a crack in the pavement
- crossing fingers
- blowing out all the candles on a birthday cake
- bridal custom of wearing something old, new, borrowed, blue

and so on.

Groups of six choose one superstition and work out a scene which shows how it became a superstition. For example, a fictional, maybe humourous story about the first time something preceeded a bad or good event, and therefore was adopted as an omen.

This can be developed further by groups polishing and refining their stories by scripting them as radio plays. They would need to work out appropriate sound effects, such as percussion instruments, ticking clocks, dripping or bubbling water, animal howls or cries, hideous laughter, screams, moans, howling winds and so on.

A Witch or Wizard Television Channel
Groups prepare one of the following programs:
- cooking
- current affairs
- news and weather (including flying conditions)
- soap opera
- advertisements
- quiz show
- fashion and beauty show
- advice segment.

Costumes

As part of the above activities, older children can design and make costumes, using simple sewing, either by hand or machine.

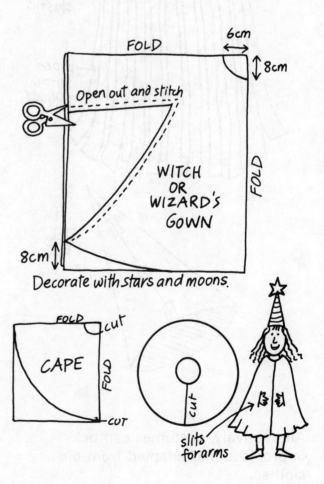

6cm

FOLD

8cm

Open out and stitch

FOLD

WITCH OR WIZARD'S GOWN

8cm

Decorate with stars and moons.

FOLD — cut

CAPE

FOLD

CUT

cut

slits for arms

If this is impossible or too difficult, children can make paper costumes out of newspaper sheets or large paper bags.

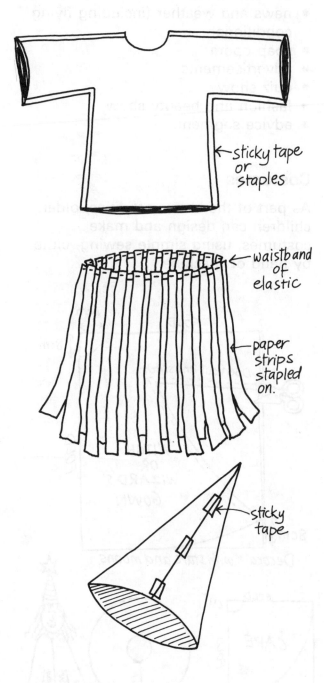

sticky tape or staples

waistband of elastic

paper strips stapled on.

sticky tape

Alternatively, costumes can be improvised and adapted from old clothes.

 Art

Identikit Pictures
Cut up magazine and newspaper pictures, and assemble identikit pictures of 'wanted witches and wizards'. Children can complete them by making them into 'wanted' posters. Reasons must be given for why the person is wanted.

Art Starter
Give each child a sheet of art paper on which you have pasted an eye or pair of eyes from magazine pictures. These can be threatening or quite benign. Children complete the picture of a witch or wizard, and then draw in a setting for the picture.

Witch and Wizard Mobiles

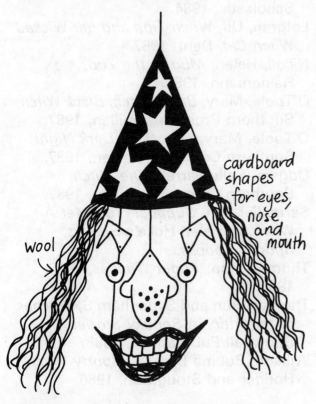

wool

cardboard shapes for eyes, nose and mouth

Create A Witch/Wizard

Create a character. Give your witch or wizard a name, and create a background for him or her.
Where was he/she born? Give family details. Give details of early magical powers. What witch school was attended? What is taught in a school like that?

Write about your character:
• a radio or video play
• a play
• a novel
• a cartoon series
• a diary written by the character
• an autobiography by the character
• a picture story book.

Make up stories about your witch character. Script some as radio plays and broadcast to the class over the school PA system. Compose chants for spells.

Create the characters as models and video the animated action in a setting constructed for the story.

Looks great!

Research

Find out about the origin of witches:
• why were these women persecuted and feared, yet turned to for help?
• herbal medicine
• witch hunts
• punishments for witches
• famous witches (Joan of Arc was burned as a witch)
• superstitions (see p. 195).

197

Bibliography

Barry, Margaret, *Simon and the Witch in School*, Collins, 1988.

Bird, Malcolm, *The Witch's Handbook*, Deutsch, 1984.

Blackie, Pamela, *Jinny the Witch Flies Over the House*, Anderson, 1984.

Chichester, Imogen, *The Witch-Child*, Kestrel, 1984.

Coombs, Patricia, *Dorrie and the Birthday Eggs*, Penguin, 1982.

Dahl, Roald, *The Witches*, Penguin, 1983.

Dugan, Michael, *Spelling List*, Southern Cross, Macmillan, 1987.

Dugan, Michael, *Spooky Riddles*, Southern Cross, Macmillan, 1987.

Gilbert, Pamela, *Gemma and the Witch's House*, Hodder and Stoughton, 1986.

Hughes, Frieda, *Getting Rid of Aunt Edna*, Piper, 1988.

Klein, Robin, *Thalia the Failure*, Ashton Scholastic, 1984.

Lofgren, Ulf, *Witch Tipp and her Wicked Witch Cat*, Dent, 1987.

Nicoll, Helen, *Mog at the Zoo*, Heinemann, 1982.

O'Toole, Mary, *Black Witch, Black Witch*, Southern Cross, Macmillan, 1987.

O'Toole, Mary, *One Dark, Dark Night*, Southern Cross, Macmillan, 1987.

Odgers, Sally Farrell, *The Witch*, Southern Cross, Macmillan, 1987.

Serraillier, Ian, *Suppose You Met A Witch*, in Helen Hoke's *Spooks, Spooks Spooks*.

Thomas, Ron, *About Witches*, OUP, 1983.

Thomas, Ron and Sydenham S, *Witches in the Attic*, in *Spooky Stories*, Snowball Publications, 1988.

Willson, Robina Beckles, *Sporty Witch*, Hodder and Stoughton, 1986.

Xylophones and Other Musical Instruments

Make A Lap Xylophone (marimba)

Pieces of wood, with wooden beaters of dowelling with a wooden bead glued on one end.

Note: length affects pitch, so that a longer bar will have a lower pitch than a shorter one. All the bars must have the same characteristics: kind of wood, moisture content.

Add as many bars as you like, to make a long xylophone that the whole class can play on at once. Make it outdoors in the playground as a permanent fixture.

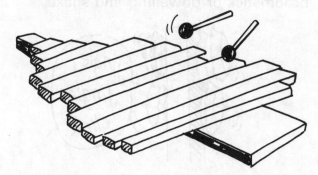

A Car Spring Gong

Suspend the spring from a scaffold, and use a metal beater to make a loud sound. A long metal bolt makes an excellent beater.

Other Gongs
Make other gongs from tin trays, painted and decorated by the children. Use metal or wooden beaters.

Suspend a metal horseshoe, and use a spoon or metal bolt for a beater.

Hang spoons and forks from a piece of dowelling, and beat them with a spoon or metal bolt.

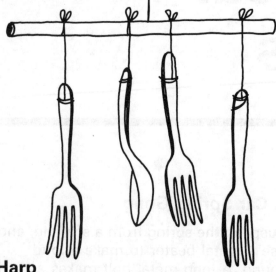

Harp

To tune the harp strings, turn the screw eye by putting a large nail through it.

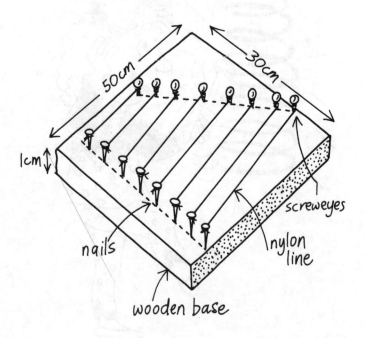

An Alternative Harp

Pull thin pieces of wire over metal or dowel rods mounted on a hollow wooden box. Strum the harp or play it with a stick.

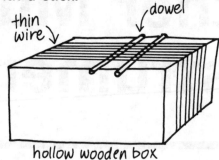

hollow wooden box

Shakers

Completely cover used light bulbs with a thick layer of papier-mache. When the papier-mache is hard, children throw the bulbs on the floor so that the glass inside breaks. Paint the shakers.

Jingle Bats

Nail bottle tops loosely to a piece of timber shaped like a bat.

Lager Phone

Attach bottle tops loosely to a broomstick or dowelling and shake.

jingle jingle clink

Tambourine

Tambourine
Use a strip of heavy cardboard. Cut four circles in the strip. String four bottle tops on pieces of string, and suspend one in each hole. Form the strip into a circle.

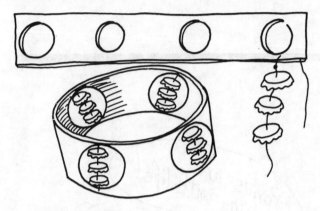

Alternative Shakers
Any plastic container half filled with beads, sand, rice, and so on. Seal the opening, and decorate.

Box Guitar

Use a wooden or cardboard box, and stretch rubber bands of different thicknesses around the box. They can be tuned by placing small pieces of wood to help stretch them tighter.

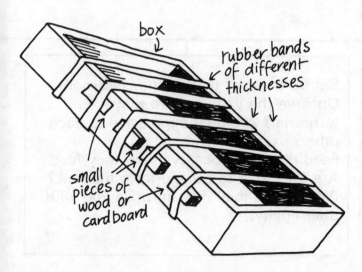

A Glassophone

Make a row of bottles, and fill them to different levels with coloured water. Try colour-coding the notes, and encourage children to write music by using the colours. Play the bottles by hitting them with a large nail, or by blowing across the openings.

You could hang them up instead...

Class Orchestra

After making, decorating and exploring the instruments, make music with the class orchestra.

Bibliography

Ardley, Neil, *Andre Previn's Guide to Music*, Macmillan, 1983.

Temmerman, Nita, *Composers Through the Ages*, Macmillan Australia Wallcharts, Macmillan, 1988.

Yabbies and Other Pond Life

Introducing Pond Life

Visit a pond. Observe. Take samples of the water. What creatures are seen? Classify and list.

Examine the water under a microscope. Can other living organisms be seen? Is there evidence of pollution?

Yabbying

Go yabbying. Take some meat and a piece of string, or make a yabby trap by making a cylinder of chicken wire and enclosing one end. Suspend the meat inside the trap near the closed end. Tie a long piece of string to the trap and throw it into the pond or dam. Children can invent and test their own yabby traps.

Ponds are teeming with life!...

Cook a large yabby. Does it look different? What does it taste like? How much do fancy dishes like yabbies and frogs' legs cost in restaurants? Find out. Compare the prices. Why are they considered to be delicacies?

Set up a yabby tank in the classroom. Observe the yabbies. Are they territorial? Are they aggressive to each other? To people?
Feed them and observe how they feed. Are they able to escape from the tank? (Watch out, they may surprise you with their agility!)

Pond Plants

Classify the plants that grow:
- in the pond
- by the pond
- on top of the water, such as reeds, water lilies.

Compare root systems, leaves, foliage, stems.

Tadpoles

Collect tadpoles and/or spawn.
Take them back to the classroom and observe them. (See p. 66)

Insect Larvae

Collect insect larvae from the pond.
Put them in a jar and observe the change from larvae to insect.
Find out what insects breed in this way.
List them.

Pond Habitat

Set up a pond habitat at school.
Dig a hole up to 1 metre deep and with shelving sides. Line it with PVA or black plastic, held in place around the edges by a ring of stones. Note: start filling it with water before you put the stones in place, or the weight of the water may tear the lining. Put oxygenating plants in the pond, in pots. Waterlilies can also be placed in pots in the pond: one waterlily plant needs approximately 1 metre diameter space. Add goldfish and reeds around the edges. Water irises can be planted in the shallow water at the edges.

Water snails and insect larvae can be placed in the pond too. Put a yabby in the pond!!

Don't let the pond get polluted.
- How can we keep it clean?
- Why should we keep it clean?

Note seasonal changes in the plants and insects. Make a photographic study of the pond over one year. Observe the activity of birds near the pond.

Zoetropes

Thaumatrope

The thaumatrope was invented by an Englishman, Dr John Ayrton Paris.
Cut 2 cardboard discs, 10 centimetres in diameter. Punch a hole each side of the discs, 6 millimetres in from the edge. Draw a picture on each disc, for a example, a birdcage on one and a bird on the other. Paste the discs together, picture side out, but one of the pictures must be upside down in relation to the other. One or both of the pictures can be a photograph or magazine picture. A light-coloured picture will show up better if the other picture is a darker contrast.

Thread one end of a rubber band through each hole and loop it through itself. Spin the disc smoothly and rapidly by holding the free end of each rubber band between a thumb and a forefinger.

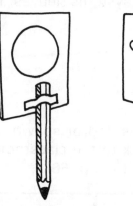

Card Thaumatrope
Two cards are illutrated as above, and taped onto a pencil. The pencil is rolled between the palms of the hands to make the pictures seem to merge.

Phenakistoscope

The phenakistoscope was invented by a Belgian, Joseph Plateau and also by Simon Ritter von Stampfer, who called his a stroboscope.

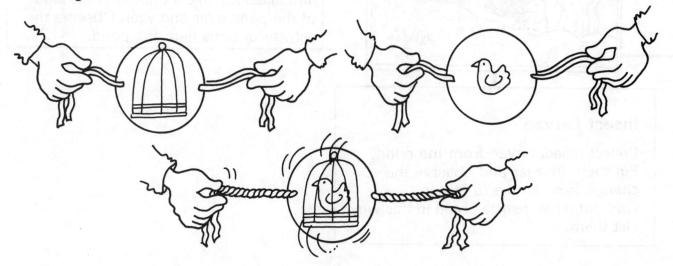

Essentially it is a disc covered with a series of evenly spaced pictures. Each picture is only slightly different from the last. When the disc is spun, the eye blends the images so that the figure appears to move.

The phenakistascope is viewed through a mirror.

Flip Book

Use a small notebook, or uniform pieces of stiff paper. Starting on one side of the first page, draw a picture. On subsequent pages, moving gradually across the pages, draw the same picture with gradual changes. When the pages are flipped, the drawing will appear to move.

Zoetrope

The zoetrope was invented by William Horner.

To make the zoetrope, enlarge the drawing below.

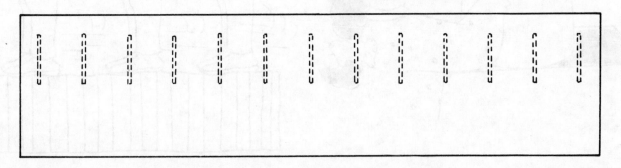

Cut the slits, and form the strip into a circle. Make a 'floor' for the cylinder by cutting and flangeing a cardboard circle, with a pinhole pierced in the centre. Pierce a pin through this into a cork with a bead on either side of the cardboard so that it spins smoothly. Put the cork in a bottle to give it weight and stand it under a light. When it is spinning, several people can look through the slits to view the moving pictures when the animation strip is inserted.

The animation strips are a series of pictures, as for the devices above. The strip is formed into a circle and is placed inside the zoetope, below the level of the slits. As the zoetrope is spun, the drawings appear to show movement.

Film Animation

Bleach old 16mm film and draw or write on it, using felt pens. Run it through a projector.

Pixilation

Using either a movie or video camera, shoot a few frames of a motionless actor. Hold the camera steady. Stop the camera, and have the actor move a step or two and freeze. Shoot a few more seconds of film, and repeat the process of the actor moving, and so on. When replayed, the effect, is that of mechanical movement; the actor appears to glide around the scene off the ground. This technique was invented by Norman Claren.

Video Animation

The video camera is mounted on a tripod for this process. Make models with clay or plasticene, or use small toys, or a combination of these. A backdrop is painted, and hung behind a tabletop on which the models and scenery are placed.

The action is created by the painstaking small adjustments made to the models in between each frame filmed.

Bibliography

Computer Software, *Animate*, Apple II Series

Index